Filling the Void: How to Overcome Addiction

by

Christopher Knippers, Ph.D.

Table of Contents

Introduction

The reasons why some people achieve long-term sobriety, and why others do not is a question that puzzles most people. It puzzles people who are in recovery, troubles friends and families of addicts, and perplexes people who work in that field. On casual observation, many things appear to be a factor. Some people think that you have to be of a certain age and/ or brain development in order to achieve long-term sobriety.

Others think that numerous severe consequences are the reason for change. The way that people have been parented is often the explanation. A popular theory is that early life trauma of a certain severity causes some people to be more resistant to recovery. There are numerous explanations and theories.

Substance Use Disorder is now widely recognized as a disease. It affects every aspect of human functioning: Physiological; neurological; psychological; social; and spiritual.

There are now numerous brain studies that show the ways in which the brains of people who have Substance Use Disorders function differently than the brains of people who do not have the disorder. Whether the drug to which the person is addicted is alcohol, narcotics, relaxants, stimulants, marijuana, or all of the above, the addicted person has similar brain functioning. The most obvious functioning brain pattern is the way that the addicted person's brain responds to their substance of choice, even in the earliest phase of the disorder. The brain of the moderate social drinker might show moderate stimulation when an alcoholic drink is presented, but the brain of a person addicted to alcohol will show extreme stimulation in the pleasure centers; and they do indeed report a kind of euphoria in the early stages of the disorder. A moderate social drinker typically reports a much milder sense of pleasure or relaxation, not euphoria; and, the moderate social drinker will not persist in drinking once he or she begins to experience the consequences of excess alcohol consumption. A true addict or alcoholic will continue their use despite even severe consequences.

The cortex is the region of the brain that helps humans make rational, logical decisions but is unable to work as well in a person who has an active Substance Use Disorder.

The cortex is under-stimulated, especially when addictive substances are present as the brain activity shifts to the central region of the brain which is the region that controls emotion and pleasure experiences. Therefore, people addicted to alcohol or other drugs can make very poor decisions. Their judgement center (frontal cortex) is temporarily impaired by the overstimulation of the central region (nucleus accumbens). Many of the recovery principles and practices followed by people who are successful in recovery actually re-wire the way the brain functions, and increases the functioning of the frontal cortex, while continuing to stimulate the pleasure centers when engaging in healthy activities.

There are also powerful reinforcement principles at work in addiction. You do not have to be an addict to understand on some level the uneasiness of experiencing a void in your life that nothing seems to fill. Everyone experiences this void to some degree, occasionally. That is what leads us to occasionally over-eat, over-spend, over-work, or to become overly involved in some other behavior. We are all attempting to fill that void with something. People with a Substance Use Disorder experience this void more intensely. The addict has learned that a drug quickly, though temporarily, fills that void. This is highly reinforcing. The connection between the use of a drug and the relief of the sense of emptiness becomes more deeply engrained with every use. That is one of the primary drivers of the continued use of a substance despite repeated severe consequences. The drug can be depended upon to relieve the stress of emptiness, as well as the stress of the severe consequences of drug use. And, as the addict becomes more isolated from any real intimacy in relationships, the loneliness exacerbates the void and drug use seems to be the only option for filling it. It becomes a vicious cycle. This is a powerful factor in drug use.

People with Substance Use Disorder also report very similar personality characteristics, ways of perceiving other people, thought patterns, and emotional reactions. For example, most people with the disorder report feeling like they do not fit in anywhere socially or culturally. They report being overly sensitive, getting their feelings hurt or their ego/pride wounded very easily. At the same time, their fragile ego strength causes them to appear self-centered and egotistical. In their attempt to compensate for their internal feelings of inadequacy they become focused on getting attention in order to validate their worth from outside themselves.

Studies show that people with Substance Use Disorders often misperceive other's emotions, and are unable to accurately assess what another person is feeling by the social cues that most people are able to accurately read. They might overlook a person's obvious facial and voice cues of either being offended, or of being pleased. They might misperceive a compliment as a manipulation. There are many other characteristics that appear in social interactions. Because of their social irregularities, some addicts and alcoholics appear similar to people who have mild autism. There are other people with substance use disorders who appear very charming and are highly skilled at social manipulation. Many studies indicate a much higher level of creativity in most addict/alcoholics than in the general population.

After a person becomes addicted, any sense of spirituality becomes disconnected or at least greatly decreased. Yet, people who successfully maintain sobriety almost all report experiencing a deep personal sense of spirituality which they maintain through prayer and meditation.

Having worked actively in the field of Substance Use Disorder treatment for over 20 years, I have witnessed many types of people achieving many different types of recovery from Substance Use Disorders. I have been very curious as I have observed people attain amazing transformations in their physical, emotional, and spiritual lives only to walk back in the door for treatment a few months later looking 10 years older than when they left months earlier, and profoundly unhappy, with a sense of being defeated. I worked at one treatment center where we thought of installing a revolving door. I grappled with how to explain what we could do better to increase sobriety time and decrease the dizzying returns to the program.

I have also observed people who appeared to be rather impulsive and who appeared to put minimal effort into their treatment, only to show up years later happily sober with their tattoos, nose rings, fuchsia hair and way too much mascara. These guys were actually happy as a clam, without having had a single relapse. It kept causing me to ask why the 19 year old minimum-wage-earner functioning with the brain capacity of a 12 year old stayed happy and sober, but the sophisticated, brilliant surgeon couldn't keep her hands off the booze for more than six months. There just seemed to be no corollaries.

That is when I set out to do some research. I put out notices to trusted leaders in the field of recovery to help me find people who had over 3 years of continuous sobriety and self-reported having happy, productive lives; and who had not ever been one of my patients, friends or co-workers. This was not as easy a sample population to find as I had originally thought. The "happy, productive life" was the characteristic that knocked some people out of the running, after just a brief conversation with them. There are unfortunately quite a number of people out there with long-term abstinence who do not qualify as "happy." At least it was a very unhappy experience for me to try to have a civil discourse with them. Fortunately, I was able, with the help of two truly amazing people who fully understand the value of being "of service," to find and complete enough interviews with a diverse sample of people to come to some excellent insights.

Those insights were insights into what makes for a successful recovery, and what actually fills that void that most people in the world are attempting to fill. I also began to fear that with my research criteria, I might be skewing the data to an older population.

That was far from being a problem as the people with over 3 years of continuous sobriety emerged, eager to share their experiences and insights. There are many people of younger generations, as well as middle age and older who are dynamic and mature in their recovery.

The people whom I interviewed were eager to share openly about their lives, their feelings, their struggles, and their triumphs. The facts that they shared with me were verified by addiction treatment professionals who maintain contact with them and are an ongoing part of their recovery journeys.

I suggested to everyone that they might want their identity disguised in some ways; however, only two of the twelve people in this population wanted anything about their identity changed. In the following pages you will read about some very diverse, dynamic lives; many of whom defy stereotypes and assumptions about Substance Use Disorder and recovery. It became very clear why some people are able to fill the void, attain long-term sobriety, and attain a happy productive life.

Their stories speak for themselves. you will see as you read about these amazing, diverse lives, that all of them have several key factors in common. After the presentation of the these individual's true life experiences, we will explore the factors that have made their lives successful, happy, and fulfilling.

The things that have helped these people find lasting recovery are things that everyone can have. With the knowledge of what has helped people find joy and fulfillment, you too can seek and find the same things.

People who do not have a Substance Use Disorder can benefit from the life experience of those who have battled that condition and found fulfillment in life. Everyone experiences the same conditions and emotions in life that addicts experience (albeit usually with less intensity) and can benefit from the ways that they have found to manage those conditions and emotions. We can all identify with experiencing the void, experiencing loss, feeling somewhat insecure, occasional anxiety and fear, sadness and depression, etc. So whether you are a person dealing with substance abuse, a friend or family member of someone who is dealing with it, or not personally affected by substance abuse, read on and find some highly effective, tested and proven means to deal with the human condition.

CHAPTER ONE
Bud

"I'm gonna change the way I'm live'n, and if that ain't enough, I'm gonna change the way I strut my stuff."

Bud is a man 85 years young who built a highly successful business as an insurance broker for the banking industry. Today he is the chairman of his own company, and works with his son who is president. He is a bright, humorous, joyful man with an infectious smile and sparkling eyes. Everyone walking past our table at the lunch rush after a large tournament at a prestigious country club stopped to share greetings and a joking comment with Bud. Even the staff of this venerable club went out of their way to pass by our table and connect with him.

I met with Bud to ask him what his secret is to success. Not in the corporate world; but in the much more global and important sense of success in life. The kind of success that makes him a beacon of joy among powerful international business men and busboys alike. The kind of success that makes him the picture of physical fitness at age 85 despite having battled several fatal diseases throughout his life. The kind of success that makes this extremely popular busy man of great stature give up several precious hours on a beautiful Southern California Saturday to talk to a little-known writer whom he had never met, just on the chance that he could help this writer find some truth to share that would help others. Bud was more than gracious and forthcoming because he devotes much of his life today to helping others.

Bud started his life in Portland Oregon, in an Irish-American family plagued with the disease of alcoholism. His father would disappear for many days at a time, and upon his return, Bud's mother would act like nothing out of the ordinary had ever happened. Some of his siblings also inherited the disease. Bud drank socially, without significant consequence, until he was in his 40's.

He joined the National Guard, took some college courses, then when he was 20 developed tuberculosis. In the 1940's, tuberculosis was not treated with the same medical advances we have today, and at best was treated with just bed rest; at worst it was commonly treated with "hard work" which of course could make it much worse.

Despite a grim prognosis, Bud managed to beat the overwhelming odds and recover after about 2 years. He was broke, with no useful education, and no prospects. He had lived in Pasadena, California since age 16 so he looked around the competitive job market of Southern California and took what work he could find; then eventually ended up working in an insurance brokerage. Through the years he became quite successful and became a partner in the firm.

In his early 40's, his formerly inconsequential social drinking was suddenly escalating out of control. He was aware that there was a serious problem, especially having come from an alcoholic family. He sought help. He relapsed after treatment, and repeated the cycle of relapse and treatment numerous times throughout his 40's. His wife had enough, and not being a very good enabler or co-dependent, divorced him. Bud continued cycles of drinking, followed by going to treatment; and somehow remained successful in business. Each time he would relapse, he just said to himself that, "Next time, I'm going to make it." Finally, in 1977, right before returning home from a business trip to London, he celebrated his latest business victory with a few drinks in the pub. He is unsure of what happened after that, but he found himself approximately a week later, back in Los Angeles not knowing how he had arrived there, or exactly what had happened for the week following his drinking in the London pub. From what he was able to learn, he had been asked to leave the fine London hotel where he had been staying for about a week, boarded a flight to Los Angeles, and ended up back home; all without any recollection of the exact events in real time.

It was this blackout drunk event that ended Bud's years of out-of-control drinking. He just simply knew that his relationship with alcohol was completely over; and from his numerous stays in rehabilitation programs, he knew what he had to do next. He got himself to an alcoholics recovery meeting, connected closely with a sponsor, surrendered to God, and began working the Twelve Steps. But more importantly, he began to change.

Change is one of Bud's primary principles of success. He stated that recovery from alcoholism actually means "CHANGE." There at our table in the country club, he sang a little tune with lyrics he said he had lived by for many years now: "I'm gonna change the way I'm live'n, and if that ain't enough; I'm gonna change the way I strut my stuff." This happens by taking an inventory of everything about ourselves that is good and has been working well for us, then hold on to those characteristics. Next, look at all of the behaviors and characteristics we have that have not worked well for us and our relationships, then change those things. True recovery happens when one becomes willing to change all of the characteristics that led to the progression of the disease in the first place.

Characteristics that Bud says will lead to success in life are: Faith; Freedom; Gratitude; Determination; Communication; Connection with others; Responsibility; Humor; and Joy.

Faith in God has always been part of Bud's life since childhood, growing up in a devout family. Even when his drinking separated him from the intimacy of a close relationship with God, he continued to pray and attend services. After he became sober, his faith took on new meaning and he said that he finds tremendous strength and comfort in his faith in God. He continues to attend the same church he has attended since he was 16 years old. Faith is essential to life and to successful recovery.

Freedom from the control of alcohol and other drugs has been liberating to Bud. It has opened up a much wider world of freedom. Freedom to be who and what he was created to be. To express his ideas freely, to freely pursue his interests, and to have the relationships he values. He considers freedom to be a gift to be sought after and protected.

Gratitude guides Bud's life. He is grateful for his sobriety and what it affords him in life. He is grateful to God, and to the people who have helped guide him. He is grateful even for the tuberculosis that nearly killed him, for the lost week of his life during the blackout drinking experience in London that could have ended tragically, for the open heart surgery he had a few years ago and for the cancer he overcame recently. Bud is a grateful man. His priest told him many years ago, in his early sobriety that, "The greatest gifts that you will ever receive are often accompanied by the greatest pain." Therefore, Bud is grateful even for the pain; because he has discovered the gifts to which the pain led.

Perhaps that is why determination has always been a driving force in Bud's life, and a characteristic which is an integral part of recovery. We can be determined to find the gift associated with he pain that we are going through; and focus more on finding the gift than on feeling the pain. Even before he was sober, Bud was determined to become sober, despite numerous failed attempts at sobriety. He said that those failures were not discouraging; and that he maintained his determination, just knowing that one day he would be sober. That determination has served him well in many areas of his life: Relationships; Health; and Business. We can all develop that dynamic driving force of determination. Just stay focused on what you want to accomplish and who you want to become.

A sense of determination helps us approach life with more energy and confidence. Gaining confidence enhances the ability to communicate. It is through learning to effectively communicate your ideas that you become more confident. Learn what you really believe in; and then develop a style of communicating those ideas effectively.

Communication and confidence help in our connection with others. It is through strong, deep, and open connection with other people that we are able to have a meaningful life. From the beginning, he recognized that in sobriety he would need meaningful connections with people; and immediately found a sponsor in his recovery program who would be open and honest with him. Despite being a highly self-confident independent man Bud knew that he was gong to have to do what his sponsor told him to do, even if he didn't want to do it. Such relationships are necessary in recovery. He values humor and some small talk, but there also has to be an element of authenticity in the relationship, in which each person also says what he or she truly believes. Bud enjoys people from all walks of life, and people with whom he disagrees, as long as they are open, honest, and respectful. These relationships of great integrity are necessary for anyone wanting to grow and experience fulfillment in life.

Having integrity in relationships is part of being responsible. Bud believes in taking responsibility for one's own life, as well as being responsible in relationships with others. He spoke of the Importance of not allowing oneself to feel like a "victim." That victim mentality is seen pervasively in today's society as is the attitude of "entitlement." Both attitudes are related to not taking responsibility for one's own life and one's own circumstances. He said that lying in bed for 2 years of misery with tuberculosis, he never allowed himself to pity himself, feel victimized, or think that he deserved better.

Instead, he took responsibility for finding ways to help himself overcome the disease. He feels the same way about alcoholism. He never blamed his father or his genetic inheritance. He merely took responsibility for dealing with what had been dealt to him.

He is responsible to himself by being responsible in how he takes care of the health that he has been given, through daily exercise and following a healthy diet. Responsibility in all areas of life is key to success in recovery.

If all of this sounds a bit heavy, it is certainly balanced with a lot of humor. Bud sees the humor in life. He sees his own foibles, the ironies in others, and some of the absurdities of the human condition as hilarious. He laughs often and freely. He said that he could not survive without seeing the humor in life. All of this humor brings him great joy.

To me, joy really defines Bud. Joy is actually the first characteristic that Bud mentioned to me as being an important factor in his success in life, which brings us back to determination and gratitude. Both lead to great joy.

The recovery principles so evident in this man's life essentially come down to a passion for life that helped him overcome the effects of growing up in a dysfunctional alcoholic family, his own disease of alcoholism, other near-fatal diseases, financial set-backs, and a host of other challenges throughout his life. He had a strength of spirit, and a determination to fulfill the potential that he believed he had, even when people and circumstances indicated otherwise. He had a strong belief in himself which overcame every obstacle. He also mentioned something else which was a constant in his life, and which I believe instilled this faith in himself: His faith in God. Even as a child growing up in an alcoholic family, he found great comfort and solace in his church, sought and nurtured that source of peace; and never broke that thread which tied him to something greater than himself, even in his darkest times. I imagine the thread of Bud's faith to which he held throughout the dark times as being much like the thread of love that Mary Oliver so eloquently describes at the end of her poem, The Return:

Half blind with weariness

I touched the thread and wept.

O, it was frail as air.

And I turned then

With the white spool

Through the cold rocks,

Through the black rocks, Through the long webs,

And the mist fell,

And the webs clung,

And the rocks tumbled,

And the earth shook.

And the thread held.

I believe that Bud's relationship with a power greater than himself, which began very early in his life, sustained him and held him through the valleys of the shadow of death.

Human connections also kept and continue to keep Bud sustained and fulfilled. He has unconditionally loved his family, has had a relationship with clergy all his life, has a sponsor to whom he listens (despite Bud's own obvious success in life), and stays in close relationship to numerous people in mutually meaningful dialogue.

Out of all the characteristics that Bud says help him in his recovery (faith, freedom, gratitude, determination, communication, connection with others, humor, and joy), I believe that the essence of his success in life and in his recovery from alcoholism is his faith, and his gratitude. I believe that all of the other characteristics have been born of those two qualities: Faith and gratitude.

CHAPTER TWO
Rhonda

"I thank God for the tough times in my life."

Rhonda is an Addictions Counselor who is happily married to her husband of over 20 years. As any couple whose marriage has survived over 20 years can say, they have had some rough times. Like the time he was in prison for felony burglary and she had to support herself as a pimp, and eventually a prostitute. And, then there was a rough patch in the marriage after she chased him around Hollywood shooting at him with a sawed-off shotgun. He pouted over that one for quite awhile, as men will do. But forgiveness seems to be the key to the longevity of their marriage.

She grew up an only child in a loving African-American family that values education, responsible professional work, God, and family. They tried to shield her from some of the harsher realities in the 1970's world of south central Los Angeles where they lived. They encouraged her to seek the better influences around her, and avoid any gang members. They wanted her to follow their example of rising above some of the darker forces that could influence you in that world.

But, her parents knew something was different about Rhonda when she was just 12 years old, and began having an upset stomach only in the mornings, along with fluctuations in energy level. They feared that the gangs had gotten to their little daughter in an even more frightening way than they had ever imagined.

Her mother took her to the doctor. Rhonda was pregnant at the age of 12. This was devastating to Rhonda; not because of being pregnant at the age of 12, but because she found out that the boy she thought was her boyfriend had only used her as a sex toy. Her parents insisted on her terminating the pregnancy. This would be the first of 8 abortions that she would have; and the beginning of her long, hard-driving, violent run of a life brought to the gates of Hell by crack cocaine and booze.

It was the 1970's, and people were experimenting with cocaine in that community. Her father had tried it, and left some in his bathroom. Rhonda found it. She had heard about it on the streets, and what a wonderful sensation it could give you. She decided to try just a little. She was instantly hooked. A whole new world opened up to her. All the tortuous pain and suffering she had felt as a sexually abused and humiliated 12 year old girl disappeared. For the next 19 years, she would spend every waking moment sacrificing whatever and whomever she had to sacrifice in order to obtain that sensation.

At 12 years old Rhonda was beginning to embrace the gang community, and let them have their way with her in order to obtain the alcohol and crack cocaine she craved. All the while, she continued to attend school, and church; and to appear to be the daughter her parents had originally hoped for. For most of her teenage years, she managed to keep her drug use and much of her gang life hidden from her parents, the school and church.

At the age of 22 she tried to turn her life around. She had married, carried a baby to full term and had given birth. This was the first time she had not used abortion as a form of birth control. It was going to be a new life, although the baby showed early signs of poor health. Her first-born baby, the hope for her new beginning, died. She was devastated. With all hope of a new life gone, Rhonda returned to crack cocaine and alcohol with much greater conviction than she had ever done before.

She married a second time, but retained her ties to the first husband. One man represented stability to her, and the other represented the free-wheeling drug life. Both men became pawns in her games for several years. Rhonda had plenty of enablers in her life. Her parents and others would continue to pick up the pieces of the life she kept breaking, and never demand any responsible behavior or commitment from her.

Rhonda had 2 healthy babies but gave them over to her parents, so that she could continue to devote her life to drugs, and the activities involved in a life focused on addiction. At age 26, it appeared to her family and others that she was trying to turn her life around when she became the church pianist. But her motive in doing that was really just to be able to live in the apartment that the church provided her. In that apartment she would be close to her drug dealers and the people with whom she used drugs. The church pianist job did not last long. It is hard to hide a church pianist on crack.

Rhonda thought she and her husband had finally found the cure for their crack addiction. It was "natural," it was said to be safe, and it was gaining wider and wider acceptance by polite society: Marijuana. They were living in a mostly Caucasian neighborhood in Hollywood surrounded by actors and others in the entertainment field, and looked like they were fitting in. For almost four years, she managed to get by mostly on marijuana, alcohol, and very little cocaine, not realizing that the marijuana was keeping her addiction alive and thriving. It was toward the end of this period that Rhonda intercepted a phone call from a woman calling her husband when he wasn't home. Rhonda, being suspicious, pretended to be her husband's sister and encouraged the woman to leave any message she wanted. Rhonda heard how passionately in love the woman was with her husband. When he returned home, Rhonda was waiting, confronted him, things escalated; and ended with her chasing him around Hollywood shooting at him with a sawed-off shotgun. He gave her a little time to cool off . . . about 6 months, before returning home. He has never strayed again.

Rhonda learned a valuable lesson from all of that: The importance of clear communication, having firm "boundaries," and enforcing them with definite consequences.

The Hollywood glamor was wearing thin, and her husband was going off to prison on felony burglary charges; so Rhonda was in the streets. She could no longer turn to her ex-first-husband, because he had killed his new wife and then himself. Her parents finally saw that her troubles were due to irresponsible decisions she had repeatedly made, and they were not going to pick up the pieces this time. They were already rearing two of her sons. She had a third young son by now, whom she was rearing by herself. She needed help just trying to survive.

Rhonda had heard of people getting a pretty sweet deal by pretending to want to get sober, going to a drug rehab program, having a place to sleep and all meals provided for a month or two. It sounded like a good deal to her, so that's what she did. Her family was so proud and hopeful! They took her son in while she went to a well- respected drug rehab program where she learned from another patient about how to get prescription opiates and ecstasy, which was much easier to get at this time than crack cocaine. After rehab, her mother picked her up and helped her daughter celebrate by toasting her with champagne. They drank together all night. Afterwards, Rhonda was right back out looking for all the drugs she could find; and ended up back in the arms of her one true love: Crack.

She met a man who was willing to help her. She had not destroyed her looks, and he could use her in his business. She was a madame to his stable of prostitutes. Rhonda decided she had learned enough about the business to start a little venture of her own; so she became the pimp, herself. She was doing well, but the amount of crack and alcohol she was using was getting expensive, and she decided to start working the streets in addition to pimping. It was a lot rougher than she had imagined. She was abused and raped; but to her it was worth it, in order to keep the flow of drugs she had to have in order to survive.

Rhonda maintained custody of her third son, even throughout her work in prostitution. They lived in a roach-infested motel room. They literally slept with roaches in the bed and stored what little food they had with roaches crawling on it. Her 8 year old son was left alone for 3 or 4 days at time in a sleazy, dirty, roach-infested motel room surrounded by drug-addicted neighbors while she would be away doing whatever she had to do to keep the drugs flowing. She didn't care who or what she had to sacrifice. She was going to stay high, no matter what.

Often it is a harsh confrontation that turns a person's life around. Rhonda had experienced many harsh confrontations throughout her 41 years; but there was something more stinging about a series of confrontations from strangers around this time that would impact her as nothing had before. Rhonda was working her corner of the street one evening, as she had done so many evenings before without incident, when a woman drove by and yelled, "You dirty, filthy whore!" There was something about that incrimination that was especially stinging to Rhonda. She could not get those cutting words out of her mind. They reverberated throughout the night. It was soon after that incident when a young man drove up saying he wanted to purchase her services. He was far from her typical john. He was young, fairly good looking, and driving a nice car. She reluctantly got in. He instantly pulled his pants down, put a gun to her head, and forced her head down on his lap. Afterward he took all her cash, told her that she would work for him from now on, give him all her money, and in return, he would not kill her. She went back out on the street, and was able to convince her next john to drive her far away from that part of the city. In fact, to another part of Southern California. She was now penniless, without the drugs she craved, not knowing what had become of her young son. She was now driven, not by drugs, but by the obsession to save her son.

Rhonda returned to Los Angeles, found her son, and begged her mother for help. This time, Rhonda was not manipulating, scamming, or scheming. She desperately wanted help. Her mother took her to a major hospital where they were going to admit her to the psychiatric ward, but could not find a psychiatrist right away to admit her. She and her mother left, and began researching rehabilitation programs that would take both Rhonda with her son and house them together in a long-term safe environment while Rhonda received treatment. They found Miriam's House that was going to open in three weeks. Until then, Rhonda would report to a facility daily to be drug tested. It worked, and she was able to live with her son in a safe, caring environment, receive treatment, and learn basic life skills, for two years.

It is now 6 years later and Rhonda has remained sober from all mood-altering substances. She is happy in her marriage, has a fulfilling career as an addictions counselor, and is proud of her 3 sons,

According to Rhonda, the keys to her ongoing success are:
Life finally became so unbearable, she had to do something different; she is actually grateful to the young man who threatened her life if she didn't work for him; her love for her sons, and her desire to be a mother to them; always praying, and seeking God, even in her addiction; and having her father finally set boundaries and enforce them.

People gave her a helping hand, and taught her life skills for two years in treatment. She forced herself to change old life style habits, such as taking the easy way out. Rhonda maintained "willingness" to stay in recovery. She remained consistent in obtaining a sponsor and attending Twelve Step support meetings. Fellowship with other women in the Twelve Step program who also understand tough times has given her a sense of grounding, validation, and support.

Rhonda's life began with the support and human connection that likely sustained her through unbelievable self-imposed adversity, and drew her back into a chance at recovery. Unfortunately, those loving family relationships also provided her with her first early exposure to drugs; as well as with the means to continue using drugs. The well- known Addiction Psychiatrist, Dr. Joseph Pursch says that without enablers, there would be no addicts. She had plenty of enablers. At the same time, Rhonda had those qualities that appear to be such an advantage in life, but which can be an addict's undoing: Charm; good looks; and an uncanny ability to manipulate people.

Perhaps that is why it took harsh confrontation to get her attention. Harsh confrontation is currently used less and less in treatment and intervention. It is not always the best way to get an addict's attention; but sometimes it is. In Rhonda's case confrontation was necessary.

Rhonda is another one who needed very long-term treatment that focused on basic life skills. She is another example of someone from a middle class upbringing who, none- the-less, had no real life skills. Today, Rhonda is putting all of her new skills to valuable use, and is leading other people to the gifts that she has experienced.

Recovery works, even for people on whom most of society have given up as hopeless.

CHAPTER THREE
Marko

"Recovery is not what I 'do'; Recovery is what I 'am."

Marko has a warm smile and seems surrounded by positive energy. The 22 year old already has 4 and a half years of being clean and sober. This was no coddled upper middle-class kid of enabling parents so often seen in treatment centers today. Marko had lived a rough life his entire life. He had more experience of a brutal world than most people ever even conceive in a lifetime. Yet here he sits at age 22, beaming with joy and eager to contribute what he can to the betterment of society.

Of German descent, living in a predominantly Hispanic town in Arizona, with a drug addicted father and a mother working two jobs to feed her young boys, Marko felt completely alone in the world. By age 7, Marko's father disappeared, abandoning the boy, his mother, and a newborn baby. Marko was old enough to feel the rage of the injustice that was being done to him and his family.

He developed a highly defensive, defiant persona. After years of being the object of ridicule and racism in that Hispanic community, with absolutely no support at home or school, he turned to gang life and drugs for a sense of identity. By age 13, he had already been arrested for marijuana possession.

His sentence for the marijuana charges was 2 years probation, during which his mother sent him to a wilderness program for troubled youth. This was a program based, not on the newer evidence-based treatments for young men with behavior problems, but on the older less effective methods of behavior modification. As is common when such methods are used on this population, Marko's rage only exacerbated; and he found ways to continue and indeed escalate his drug use in that program. From the ages of 13 to 18, Marko became highly addicted to cocaine. He felt as though this was the answer to all of his problems. He loved the sense that all was right with the world and himself.

During this period, Marko had multiple arrests and multiple treatments. He shut his mother out of his life, not wanting to be close to anyone outside the drug culture. He managed to complete a High School equivalency degree (GED); but his focus remained on drug use.

By age 16 Marko's father had returned to his life and became his drug buddy. Father was also very abusive; but Marko craved attention from his father and was willing to put up with the abuse in order to have his father in his life. By age 17, Marko had accepted his life as an addict and gang member. That is just what he was, and he was resigned to that life, however short it may end up being. Marko said that all of his perceptions of the world had become drastically skewed, and that eventually the only thing in life that he valued at all was drugs.

At 18 Marko was doing everything under the influence of drugs. His system was drug- ridden 24 hours a day, 7 days a week. He had been driving in a blackout and physically fighting with his life-long friend, when he dropped his friend off at his friend's car. The friend drove away, hit another car, killing a young father, gruesomely disfiguring the young mother, and injuring the little child. Marko's childhood friend is still serving a 21 year prison sentence. Following this incident, Marko went into a deep depression, and also developed pancreatitis. He decided it was time to reconcile with his mother. He went to see her and she welcomed him home.

His mother had heard of New Life House and sent Marko there. He arrived an emotionally broken yet highly defensive, hardened teenager with no clue of a life other than one filled with drugs and abusive relationships. It would take awhile to develop any semblance of trust. The one thing Marko did accept from the beginning was that he needed to change.

Right away, Marko noticed a difference in this program from the numerous others to which he had been. Instead of constantly telling him what not to do, the staff and his peers were instructing him in what to do differently . . . how to live life. In all of his 18 years, he had never had anyone to show him how to be a successful human being; and for the first time in 18 years he was willing to learn. He started by taking responsibility for the way he was thinking, and the choices he had made. Marko could no longer be a "victim."

He no longer blamed his past nor anyone in it, for what had become of him. He became humble for the first time in his life. Since arrogance and the defiance that goes along with it is incompatible with sobriety, his counselors and peers reinforced humility in him. Marko had always defiantly resisted any hint of being humble or submissive; so in order to teach him that he could be humble and still be okay, they gave him special assignments and duties that would cause him to take a submissive role in the therapeutic community.

One such assignment was to be the "lighter boy." For a period of time, anytime a peer would say, "Hey, lighter boy, light my cigarette!" this former rough tough gang member had to quickly respond by rushing over to light the peer's cigarette. To help Marko with his resistance to being close to people, he was enrolled in the "hug program." People could walk up and hug him at any time, and he could not resist. He also was taught the most basic of life skills, such as keeping a clean tidy room, laundered clothes, balanced meals and exercise.

Gradually, Marko began to accept that he needed internal change, rather than trying to change everything and everyone around him. He slowly opened up and began talking to people about his thoughts and feelings. He was starting to become excited by healthy living, rather than the rush of rebellion.

There was one aspect of this new life style with which Marko really had trouble. He heard everyone around him talking about a Higher Power, and the advantage of prayer. This was totally foreign to him. He could not understand it, he was frustrated by the whole idea of a God, and was a little angry. His life was already so much better. He was feeling happier, had more energy, had true friends; but he struggled to understand what this Higher Power was. He was tired of people telling him to just get on his knees and pray, but one day he did; and here is his simple prayer: "F--- Dude! Just help me, here!" That did it! Marko finally understood and accepted that Higher Power was part of his new life. That is not a prayer that you will find in your church's liturgy; but in Marko's case, it worked! Marko came to understand Higher Power as, "The understanding that I cannot be in ultimate control. There is more experience to be had, more to understand, more to improve on. That power has a path . . . a plan for me. I see now that I have always been taken care of. Faith is letting go to that power."

Eventually, his mother came for a visit to see how things were going this time in treatment. For the first time, Marko sat down with his mother, looked her in the eyes, and shared openly and honestly with her. After 15 minutes, she began to cry. It was as if she was meeting her son for the first time.

Marko was beginning to see life as an "experience rather than a consequence." He was excited about living for the first time. Even the setbacks and disappointments were seen as interesting rather than frustrating. After 2 years of sobriety, he believed that he was cured, and could break out on his own, away from the support that had helped him through the rough times.

He tried life away from the recovery support on which he had come to depend. Soon he discovered that it was impossible to stay focused on the practice of recovery. He had become totally focused on the gifts of recovery. Life soon became confusing and overwhelming. Marko again sought out the community that had helped him find life in the first place; and resumed practicing the steps of recovery in his daily life.

Fulfillment is now found in helping play a part in other people's transformational process, and in genuinely caring for people's welfare, in addition to caring about himself. Struggles in life are of value to him. It is all part of the gift of new life; and Marko is genuinely grateful, because each situation is put into his life for a good reason. "Recovery is not what I 'do,' it is what I 'am.'"

Marko had the opportunity to put that philosophy into action when he finally saw his father again. Though this man had abused and abandoned Nick, as well as setting the example of how to live like a craven addict, Marko apologized to his father for specific wrongs that he believed he had committed against his father. His father cried for the first time in Marko's life. They hugged each other. Marko was finally free. "Relationships are never a one-way street," according to Marko. He always looks at his own part in any relationship dysfunction.

The whole range of emotions still arise; but he has learned to look deeper than what he is feeling in the immediate situation. Often, it is fear beneath anger or sadness, so he faces the fear instead of reacting to the anger. Often, it is a matter of identifying what he can do differently. "I just identify the feeling, the thought behind it, and then figure out what I need to do differently."

In answering the question, "How could someone so completely without guidance since childhood, whose body, mind and sprit had been so scrambled by drugs for 11 years, come to such a mature understanding of himself and life," Marko answered, "Any person has the ability to tap into the understanding of care, concern, honesty . . . it is their choice."

Marko now uses his passion for helping people transform their lives by helping young adolescents who are struggling with the disease of addiction in a treatment program for adolescents.

If ever anyone had an "excuse" to remain a bitter addict, sober or not, Marko did: Abandoned; socio-economically disadvantaged; abusive addicted male role model; victim of racism since childhood; no school or community support; and a series of ineffective exploitive treatments. Against these odds, with a brain that had never been allowed to develop at all normally and was likely damaged, Marko made a choice to seek a new way of living life. His whole identity had become that of a criminal drug addict; and he accepted that as his life. He very probably had Post Traumatic Stress from the abuse he had suffered all of his life, as well as witnessing his only close friend kill someone in a drunk driving incident. Never-the-less, Marko made a choice to try a different path, and see where it led.

The power of choice is an essential component of Marko's guiding philosophy of life. Everyone has the potential within themselves to be a positive, responsible person; and is capable of making a choice to be that person, regardless of what they experienced in the past. This belief can become the basis for judgment of others' choices; but in Marko's case, it has become the basis for helping bring out that positive person through persistent care, support, and sometimes forgiveness.

In order to be consistent with this philosophy, Marko takes responsibility for his part in any conflict or struggle. Humility is a lesson he learned well, early on. He has discovered how refusing to be a victim frees him to move forward with his life, rather than being stuck in misfortune.

He, like all of these success stories in recovery, keeps his focus on other people, rather than himself. He learned the hard way how taking the gifts of recovery and trying to use them to go about his own selfish pursuits led him right back to old ineffective behavior patterns. He came to the realization that it is not about the gifts of recovery but rather it is about the practice of recovery. He also learned the difference between just doing the right things, and actually becoming the right person. In other words he integrated the 12-Step philosophy into his very being . . . his identity; rather than just going through the motions of Step 1, Step 2, Step 3, etc.

He now knows the importance of community. The same community that taught him the instructions for how to live life, keeps him on track in life, and he is open with them about what he is feeling and thinking.

His formula for managing difficult emotions is: Identify the feeling; understand the thought behind it; then figure out what I need to choose to do differently. This method is actually backed up by research as the most effective method we know in the field of psychology. It is certainly working for Marko. Another part of that formula is letting go of control.

Letting go of control is integral to Marko's understanding of Higher Power. It is a bit of a lesson in spirituality that Higher Power was revealed to Marko, not through lofty liturgy, but rather through what many would consider to be a crude, possibly even unacceptable way to approach God. What can honestly be said about Marko's initial approach is that it was deeply sincere. Sincerity is a quality that he exudes.

Anything is possible.

CHAPTER FOUR
Hal

"Deal openly and honestly, from the beginning, with the psychological aspects of the disease, and you will avoid much needless suffering."

The water was that amazing interplay of deep royal blue, blue-green, and an almost lavender hue. You could reach out and literally touch the rainbow assortment of tropical fish swimming by the yacht through the crystal clear waters. Beautiful people were draped languidly around the decks drinking in the sun under gloriously clear skies with billowy white clouds. The legendary Greek shipping tycoon graciously furnished Hal and his other guests with every reason to be happy in those moments of time when they were on board his sprawling yacht. Life seemed perfect in those moments. Living in the Bahamas, and traveling the world with the rich and famous kept Hal distracted, and at times anesthetized from the deep inner pain of his life.

That pain had plagued him since as far back in his life as he could remember. Even when he was a child in Ohio with a most common last name. He never felt good enough; never felt like he fit in. It was a constant feeling of being out of place. Children of alcoholics often grow up with that feeling. It was his mother who spent her time intoxicated. His father rarely drank; and his mother eventually started attending Twelve Step recovery meetings, and remained sober. However, Hal continued to sense that there was something deficient about him, no matter how much he accomplished. He was uncommonly handsome, and had a glamorous social life. He attained success at everything he set out to accomplish, from graduating with honors from a prestigious university to managing some of the world's finest resorts in his early 20's.

He was very young to have the responsibilities of being in charge of running every aspect of an ultra high end 2000 acre mega-resort catering to the wealthiest, most discriminating travelers of the world; but that is what he did with great success. His clientele was so impressed with him until they even accepted him into their personal social circles. His charm, outgoing personality, and high fashion cool casual appearance belied the fear, anxiety, and drive to excel accompanied by the sense of never being good enough that obsessed his mind every waking moment.

His overwhelming stress was starting to effect his health. Even in his 20's, this healthy- happy-appearing young man was being advised by his medical doctor that he had to do something to relieve the stress. His doctor advised drinking to take the edge off his stress. This was good news to Hal's boss who had been concerned that Hal was giving the wrong appearance in that industry by being a tea-totaler. Hal had not wanted to repeat the mistakes and subsequent struggles of his mother; but he reluctantly took his doctor's advice. And, though distasteful to him at first, sure enough, drinking rapidly became a great relief to him. He could look forward to taking a break from feeling the daily stress, every afternoon and evening; but soon learned that he could have that relief by drinking all day.

His drinking progressed so rapidly, until just 3 years after beginning his doctor's treatment for stress, he started developing alcohol-related kidney problems, resulting in a series of surgeries over the years. Christmas was a time of unbridled drinking, as it seemed to fit in with what everyone was doing in celebration. However, on Christmas of Hal's 31st year, he suddenly felt completely desperate after another evening of uncontrolled drinking. Hal felt completely helpless and out-of-control. He fled to his office, fell down on his knees and prayed, "God! Help me!"

Suddenly he was bathed in white light, was lifted up off the floor to his feet, and he lost the desire to drink for the next 12 years.

Hal continued his successful career, and his glamorous jet-setting social life as a sober man. As the benefits of sobriety, he enjoyed improved health, and the fellowship he experienced in the Twelve Step recovery meetings. But, while much of his anxiety had abated, Hal still had a sense of sadness and depression; as if something was still missing from his life.

This depression would lead to a couple of relapses in which Hal would know that drinking was wrong and would lead to a bad end for him; but he would do it anyway in the despair of his depression. He was still driven to "be the best;" a tendency which he said was never instilled in him by his parents, but one with which he was burdened anyway. Each relapse on alcohol would result in Hal having a relapse of his kidney and other serious health issues. Then he would go back to recovery meetings, sober up, and start the slow progression to health, again.

Finally, Hal reached a point in his recovery that he surrendered his will to the 12 Step program and a stable, devoted sponsor whose guidance he followed implicitly. He has been successfully sober for many years, now.

Hal believes that the answer to successful recovery is in staying very close to the fellowship of the Twelve Step recovery program. The more often you attend meetings, the more successful you are. Taking each of the Twelve Steps seriously, and sincerely working each of the steps is key to success. Having a sponsor whom you trust and to whom you will listen is essential. "The more you become involved, the more accepted you feel." Hal now feels accepted and is filling that sense of a void in his life through relationships within the 12 Step program.

One more thing Hal believes strongly at this point, is that everyone in recovery should deal openly and honestly from the start with all of the psychological aspects of the disease of alcoholism. He knows that dealing early on with his depression, his anxiety, and his obsession to excel would have prevented many years of emotional and physical suffering. He knows of no alcoholic or addict who does not have significant emotional baggage. It is just part of the tapestry of the disease; and part of the results of the disease. Deal with the emotional baggage that is part of the disease.

Then you will be truly free; and you will avoid much needless suffering.

Hal's recovery has had it's rewards. His 3 adult children have not had to suffer any of the pain that he has suffered, due to the fact that Hal chose to be in recovery. Hal is close to his children, close to his former wife, and close to his sponsor in Twelve Step recovery. Now, in his 70's, Hal is still working hard on personal growth, and is living back in the beautiful Caribbean.

The early signs of alcoholism appeared in Hal as a child through "a deep inner pain," even though he did not actually like alcohol until his doctor encouraged him as an adult to drink more. Hal was also burdened with the characteristics that plague most children of alcoholics: Perfectionism; never feeling good enough despite high achievement; feeling out of place. He had a role model of both alcoholism and recovery, as well as a supportive family, which likely gave him an advantage in his overall recovery.

His experience with Higher Power is both profound, and familiar to many alcoholics: Falling to his knees in desperation and finding Higher Power. This kept him sober for 12 years, until that old familiar sense of a void in his life began to overwhelm him. This void is something that most people with the disease battle;

but after he figured out that he had to stay close to the support of the Twelve Step program and his sponsor, he found that void start to fill with a sense of acceptance and belonging so often reported by others in the program.

Hal's message of facing and dealing with the emotional baggage of the disease is his greatest lesson. He believes that the Twelve Step program is necessary but not sufficient to deal with the emotional component of the disease, and requires the help of a professional. He hopes that people in recovery will not hesitate to do whatever is necessary to find emotional peace, and avoid years of needless suffering.

CHAPTER FIVE
Sebastian

"The key to happiness is service to others."

Looking at him today, at age 23, you would think that Sebastian had led a comfortable, maybe even privileged upper middle class life. He is well dressed, well groomed, polite, and speaks with confidence and intelligence. It is almost impossible to believe that he was the person he claims to have been just 3 years earlier.

Sebastian had grown up in a close loving family. He was well-liked at school, played sports, and enjoyed the relationships with his parents, his older sister, and his older half- brother. His brother was a real star. It seemed his brother was practically perfect in every way; but rather than being jealous, Sebastian was proud. The family was excited when his brother went away to college at Berkley when Sebastian was 12; but that is when life changed dramatically for Sebastian and his entire family.

The brother had discovered the Berkley drug culture and loved it. He rapidly went from squeaky clean all-

American boy, to insatiable drug addict within months. He was so desperate and filled with shame, until he attempted suicide. In the course of attempting suicide he survived, but was permanently paraplegic from his injuries.

As pressure mounted on the family his parents began having trouble in their marriage. Around age 12, Sebastian discovered relief from the pressures and extreme disappointments at home, when friends introduced him to marijuana. He also discovered a new social group that gave him a sense of belonging as his family ties began to unravel. By age 15, his parents had split up, he was living with his mother whom he had convinced to allow him to drink and smoke marijuana at home, and his sister introduced him to drug-fueled parties with the older kids in high school. He was off and running.

Sebastian never met a drug he didn't like. Around this time, OxyContin was becoming common as more and more doctors were freely passing it out to their patients. Sebastian was particularly fond of Oxy. He discovered a profitable business which would help him afford his expensive habits and addictions. He began dealing a variety of drugs out of his home. He was caught, charged with multiple felonies, and placed on probation.

The first thing he did after getting caught was, he got high. The next thing he did was go to treatment, with a strong desire to get off of OxyContin.

Sebastian had no intension of going off of alcohol and marijuana. A very common belief among addicts, and increasingly in general society, is that alcohol and marijuana are so different than opiates that you can stop doing opiates but not have to worry about completely stopping alcohol or marijuana. Sebastian soon found that this belief was a near-fatal fallacy, as so many other addicts have also discovered. (Or, as their families discovered after the addict's death.) A drug is a drug is a drug, whether it is alcohol, marijuana, opiates, muscle relaxants, or nicotine. The same part of an addict's brain that craves an opiate is triggered with any drug they ingest. Once the brain feels the pleasure of the alcohol, marijuana, or other drug, it begins to crave the strongest substance it can get.

Not only did Sebastian soon find himself trying "just a little" Oxy, he ended up injecting heroin, and doing methamphetamine. After becoming addicted, getting arrested, going to treatment, but still continuing to escalate in his drug use, Sebastian at the young age of 20, was feeling completely hopeless and helpless. One night in a drug-filled haze he suddenly felt extreme pain, noticed bleeding, and felt like he was dying. He slowly was. He called his father, was taken to the emergency room of a local hospital, and they were able to save him from the extreme damage he had done to his gastrointestinal system. After that incident he was desperate to get off all drugs; but he still resisted going to treatment.

His father prevailed, and Sebastian reluctantly went to New Life House where he saw other young men like himself, with the same disease, who had somehow transformed their lives and were happy, healthy productive members of society. Without the numbing effects of drugs, Sebastian suddenly felt shame for what he had done and what he had become. However, he also felt a sense of relief and a sense of hope for the first time. He could see that others had been able to turn their lives around. Maybe he could, too.

He would soon begin a journey that would transform his life from a lost, hopeless 20 year old drug addicted felon, to a happy, healthy, inspiring light in the frenetic world of Los Angeles. The transformation started with having a father who picked his nearly dead son up off the floor of a drug den, continued with other recovering addicts Sebastian's age who surrounded him with love, guidance, and support; and catapulted forward with

Sebastian making his own decision to turn completely away from his old life and embrace a new one.

Sebastian would never return to any of his old friends, or any other remnants of his old addict life style. He decided to completely embrace the recovery community, go against his own ego-driven impulses, and follow the principles of the 12-Step philosophy.

Sebastian has started getting high again. This time, he says he is getting high from being of service to others. Knowing his tendency to be selfish and self-centered, he resists his selfish urges and turns his attention toward looking for ways in which he can give a helping hand to someone else. He described a sense of pleasure that is literally visceral whenever he is in the process of giving assistance to other people.

A sense of gratitude floods Sebastian the way that shame and hopelessness used to flood him when he reflects on his life. This sense of gratitude is closely related to his sense of a Higher Power in his life. He believes that God's will for him is to be of service to other people, so in acting on this belief it keeps him in a constant loop of gratitude, fulfillment, and service. Sebastian said that all of this just came to him without much effort, after he made the choice to embrace a new life. No none had to talk him into believing a certain way. It all fell into pace for him when he surrendered his self-will and turned his attention toward others. It has been common for him to see other recovering addicts struggle with the whole concept of a Higher Power; but Sebastian found that being of service to others naturally guided him into a profound understanding of God. He suddenly believed and felt that everything is going to be okay.

Sebastian has an ongoing sense of confidence that everything is working out as it needs to in his life, regardless of what is happening at any given moment. His life is going to end up where it needs to end up. Though it could sound like he is in denial about the ways of the world and the vagaries of human emotion, living in a sort of 12- Step bubble, he is not. Sebastian reports having the whole range of human emotion: The shock, the alarms, the disappointments, the anger, the joy, the sadness that all of us feel as we journey through life. What sets Sebastian apart from the many people who get thrown off course due to extreme emotion is that he always catches himself before he is side-tracked. Sharing his emotions with peers and a 12 Step sponsor helps keep him balanced. Acceptance of the emotion and the situation that triggered it is also essential to his recovery. Sebastian also remembers to always look at his part in bringing about whatever upsets him in life, he takes responsibility for the situation, and he makes amends to people when needed. In so doing, he returns to the center of his belief system that regardless of outward circumstances, everything is working together for the ultimate good in life.

He also believes in the ultimate good within other people, regardless of their current behavior. He believes that everyone has a spark of good within them. For some this spark is hidden very deep within, but it is there.

If a hopeless, desperate 20 year old addict had the potential to make such a phenomenal transformation in a relatively short period of time, it seems that someone could have reached out to him long before he ended up nearly dead in an emergency room, and could have gotten help for him, sooner. Sebastian disagrees. He said that his life needed to proceed with all of the horrific consequences that occurred, otherwise he would not have been ready to make the dramatic changes that he did. An intervention would have been futile. He is grateful for all that led him to the new life that he is now experiencing.

Sebastian's experience illustrates many truths about addiction and recovery. While it seems clear that he had the genetic predisposition for addiction, he had the advantage of a solid foundation in life through close family bonds and a supportive community.

This is certainly not the case with many addicts.

Unfortunately, his family bonds were significantly strained and almost torn apart at a very vulnerable stage of life. It was doubly unfortunate that he and his sister chose to cope with the family turmoil brought on by their brother's drug use, through using drugs themselves. His fate was sealed by his successfully manipulating his mother into allowing him to openly drink alcohol and smoke marijuana at home, further convincing himself that it was a good idea to use these substances.

It was a very short step from using alcohol and marijuana over to using other drugs. Parents sometimes think that it is better to have their kids using at home than someplace else completely unsupervised; but that is like playing Russian roulette with the fragile developing adolescent brain. The brain's judgement center (the frontal cortex) is not developed enough in adolescence to make the best judgements about how to manage these powerful and potentially deadly substances;

especially when the brain is already predisposed to the addiction cycle that is triggered the first time the amygdala is stimulated by mood-altering substances.

The brain doesn't develop normally when mood-altering substances are introduced during adolescent brain development, so making decisions such as "It's a good idea to deal drugs out of my mom's home," seems perfectly logical. Consequences do not have much impact or even register with most any adolescent brain, especially after drugs have taken over the pleasure center; and a drug arrest is not likely to have a big impact, or even give a clue that the arrest was a consequence of the drug use. As in Sebastian's case, the consequences have to be extreme. Until then, there is no true willingness to change.

The consequences most likely to get attention for most any addict at any age is a consequence that dramatically conflicts with a person's dearly held sense of identity. His identity was devastated by being weak and vulnerable, with his youthful charm gone. Many addicts don't get the message, even at age 50+ that their "youthful charm" is gone ; but in Sebastian's case lying broken and bleeding on the floor, it was impossible to be in denial.

While Sebastian believes that an intervention prior to these consequences would have been fruitless, intervention was effective and necessary after he reached out to his father for help. It took the insistence of his father to get him into an effective program, because though Sebastian himself realized that he needed help, he had no idea the degree to which he needed help. His ability to reason was damaged. The people around him did realize what help he needed. Very few addicts of any age are capable of seeing themselves objectively. That ability is impaired by the substance use.

Another necessary step in Sebastian's complete recovery was being given living examples of young people in recovery with whom he could relate and identify.

Research is showing that the brain has something called "mirror neurons" which cause us to closely identify and connect with others who are similar to us. This process of mirroring can help us learn new behaviors (positive or negative), and even take on whole new ways of thinking, feeling and behaving. This is what helped Sebastian relatively quickly go from being a hopeless, advanced-stage drug addict at an early age to a happy committed young man in recovery.

The new group with which Sebastian had come to identify, had to completely replace his old group and any remnants of his old life. At his stage of development, he could not take the chance of re-identifying with anyone from the drug culture and possibly begin mirroring their behavior again. With his neurobiological predisposition to drug craving and the behavior patterns that had already been deeply ingrained for the vast majority of his life, he had little chance of survival returning to his old environment.

Guiding principles are necessary for anyone to live a fulfilling, productive life; and one of the primary reasons for Sebastian's phenomenal success in overcoming a deadly disease and living with such amazing maturity at age 23 is the guidance he receives from identifying with and and following the 12-Step philosophy. He reports finding true meaning and fulfillment through this philosophy. An essential component of this philosophy that helps Sebastian is the importance of service to others. Helping and supporting other people in their life challenges gives Sebastian a sense of the eternal, and he actually reports a physical sensation that he describes as "high" when he is of service. Other components of this philosophy that help Sebastian excel in his recovery are accepting what happens in his life (even the disappointments) without judgment, sharing his emotions with his support system, and being grateful for his new life.

Sebastian sees the good in life, in himself, and in others at all times and in all situations.

This is his mind-set, and this belief system is bringing him success, joy, and peace.

CHAPTER SIX
Deirdre

"No matter what happens in my life, the only question I ask is not, 'why me'; but rather, 'How can I become a better person through this?"

Life started in a peaceful Irish town with a prominent surgeon father and a highly respected psychiatrist mother. Deirdre was a bright-eyed beautiful child, garnering the admiration of all who met her. People of that region of Ireland held her family in the highest regard. Highly educated professionals were greatly esteemed in that culture; and Deirdre was the child of two doctors. Being bright and beautiful, from a wealthy respected family, Deirdre grew up being admired, and often envied, by all who knew her.

What was going on behind the stately walls of that Irish estate, would shock the people who so profoundly revered that family, if they had known what was really happening in that family. Deirdre spent her early childhood days in the care of nannies who tended to her basic needs; then her mother would arrive home, and despite her mother's heavy drinking each evening and her demands for Deirdre to wait on her after the servants left for the day, Deirdre felt a sense of safety with her mother present. There was no nurturing by her imperious mother; but at least she was not going to be abusive. She was predictable. It was quite a different story when the surgeon arrived later in the evening. He could be sullen and isolated; or at other times, Deirdre could find herself dodging fine china being hurled past her head, as she cowered in fear of what this capricious maniac might do next. Her life felt unpredictable and scary.

As she began school, she continued to be the focus of admiration of the community; and school offered some relief from the chaos of home. Despite all the admiration, Deirdre never completely felt at ease, and certainly never felt any sense of confidence. Then one day, at the age of 8, her mother calmly, unemotionally, announced to Deirdre that her father had dropped dead of a heart attack. Nothing more was said, there were no tears, and it was not spoken of again for 8 more years. Life went on. All that Deirdre felt was an overwhelming sense of relief. "The dragon had been slain."

Mother's drinking continued to escalate, and she continued being somewhat aloof, demanding, and imperious; but Deirdre still took comfort that mother was a predictable presence in her life. Deirdre continued to develop into a stunning, popular adolescent girl; and continued to feel increasingly insecure about herself. It felt as though she could never be "enough." She looked at the accomplishments of her family, going back several generations, and believed she could never live up to the family reputation. At the age of 16, her mother would make another announcement about her father that would be another blow to Deirdre's confidence, and create a growing sense of shame within her.

Dr. M had not dropped dead of a heart attack. He had fashioned a noose out of a neck tie, and hanged himself in the family home. Mother had discovered him, and with the family's considerable influence, was able to keep the details of his death a secret. Deirdre felt a sense of devastation. Shame began to flood her. The admiration of the masses seemed to mock what she believed to be true about her: She was a rejected, shameful girl. She had grown up with a father who did not like her and daily threatened her safety; then he brought the ultimate shame on her by killing himself in a gruesome way. In her perception, if her own father did not love her, and he actually disliked her to the degree that he wanted to escape her completely, she must be a shameful person.

Deirdre sought help from her psychiatrist mother as to how to manage her overwhelming anxiety. Her mother advised her to drink alcohol for anxiety relief. She took her mother's advice (after all, she was a psychiatrist) and began to treat her anxiety with "a few drinks." She soon learned that for her, even at age 16, there was no such thing as "a few" drinks. Deirdre drank to get drunk. Each time, feeling more and more shame, and a growing sense of darkness inside her, but she continued drinking anyway.

In her early 20's, she thought that escaping the darkness of her childhood and adolescence could be accomplished by a move to the United States. She settled in the western US. Her beauty and Irish charm opened doors in a famous city where beauty is valued above all else. She was able to find work in the hotel industry, eventually working her way up to hotel management. The work was going well; but the compulsion to drink that she had hoped to leave behind her in Ireland followed her relentlessly to the United States.

She met a handsome clergyman who had recently become a psychologist. He wanted to help her. He took control of her at a time when her drinking was causing her life to spin out of control. He seemed to be exactly what she needed for stability at that time. What good fortune to meet a man with both spiritual and psychological depth! They quickly fell in love, married, and began a happy life in a beach cottage. She continued to manage a hotel, and he established a successful psychology practice.

Her drinking did not subside for long. She soon found that her husband's method of "helping" her with her drinking problem involved escalating his control of her every move; and eventually involved hitting and punching her, repeatedly. The hell of her childhood was nothing compared to the hell of her marriage. She was alone in life, away from the friends and family of her Irish home, her drinking increasingly out of control, and dependent on a man who tortured her. At the same time, she blamed herself because of her out-of-control drinking; but no matter what she tried, she simply could not stop. It only got worse when she tried.

She divorced the clergyman-turned-psychologist after a year. His particular approach to religion and psychology was not working for her. Sadly, having that abusive husband out of her life did not prevent her drinking from escalating. Her world was one of depression, shame, fear, and despair, as she struggled to keep her head above water every moment of every day, and trying to continue to function in a responsible job.

Eventually, out of desperation, she accepted the ex-husband back into her life.

This time, his approach was to try to control her with money, and distract her with world travel. They traveled the world, staying in 5-star resorts in exotic lands. Deirdre's drinking was beginning to produce terrifying hallucinations. After awhile, she did not know whether she was in Malaysia or Martinique. Every new luxury resort only looked and felt like another frightening nightmare. In a moment of clearer thinking, in one of the Asian countries that they visited, Deirdre went to a prayer wall where the Buddhist faithful of that country were leaving written prayers on the wall; and she wrote a prayer saying that she simply wanted to be happy. Happiness did not come instantly; and eventually, the ex-husband gave up on his money and world-tour cure to her problems, and they again parted ways.

Back in the beach cottage and in hotel management, Deirdre settled into a life of working, and drinking. She had given up on ever being the educated successful person that all other members of her family had been, though it still troubled her that she was by comparison such a failure.

New Years Eve, 1983, Deirdre was walking down her driveway toward her cottage carrying a gallon of cheep wine, when a neighbor confronted her and said, "Don't you think it's time you stopped drinking and started going to AA?" Deirdre was a bit taken aback by the woman's bluntness. She barely knew her, but obviously the neighbors had noticed Deirdre's problem. Deirdre had tried such meetings many years before, but had long-ago decided that she was "not one of those people." However, upon her neighbor's gentle confrontation, Deirdre simply responded, "Yes."

As she timidly slipped into the musty florescent-lit room in the basement of an old civic building on that New Years Eve feeling terrified, desperate, and all alone in the world, a haggard, toothless old man gently approached her and said, "You are welcome here." Instantly, this beautiful, young woman who had grown up in prestige and privilege, but who none-the-less never felt the feeling of fitting in or being "enough," suddenly felt that she was safe, that she fit in, and that she was indeed enough; all because of a haggard, toothless old man in a dingy basement caring enough to reach out to her with a sincere, kind word and warm greeting. She was finally in a place where no one cared about her status, her beauty, whether or not she was educated or successful. She could simply "Be," and know that she was accepted the way she is. It is the year 2013, and Deirdre has never tasted alcohol or other drugs since that New Years Eve, 1983.

She continues to attend Twelve Step recovery meetings, and works the Twelve Steps, finding that the most essential for her is to daily take her own Inventory. One of the primary reasons for her sustained sobriety is that she never allows herself to feel like a "Victim." Whenever something difficult or disappointing happens, she doesn't turn to blaming anyone or anything, present or past. Instead, she simply says to herself, "How can I become a better person; and how can I find a solution to this?"

The importance of qualified professional help for her life-long battle with depression and anxiety became clear as Deirdre began to progress in her recovery and was able to trust a psychology professional. This has been a major boost to her success in recovery.

Deirdre has discovered a relationship that is the most sacred, intimate relationship imaginable. She has discovered a deeply intimate relationship and communication with God, through meditation and contemplative prayer. She sits in the presence of God daily and just listens for guidance, or anything else God wants for her to experience in that time and space. Part of Deirdre's recovery program is to stay close to other people who have also discovered this beautiful, enlightening, intimate relationship with God.

Her relationship with God is the most essential part of Deirdre's success in recovery.

Today, Deirdre is happily living in her beach cottage, working for a major corporation, and enjoying the fellowship of friends in recovery. No longer driven by the desires for high achievement or material gain, Deirdre seeks and has found peace.

Deirdre had the perfect storm of factors that came together to create a life of dependence on alcohol which was fueled by depression and anxiety: Genetic predisposition; role models of alcoholism; child abuse; family shame; family secrets; and even "professional/ maternal" advice to drink as solution to teenage anxiety. All of the prestige, money, charm and beauty she possessed could not protect her from the ravages of the disease. She also suffered from what children of alcoholics, as well as alcoholics report as never feeling like they are "enough"; and the feeling of "never fitting in."

Geographic moves, no matter how far away, are rarely a solution until the disease itself is addressed. In Deirdre's case, the repetition compulsion (the tendency to repeat childhood situations) followed her to the United States from Europe, with heavy drinking, an abusive relationship with a man, and the disappointing pursuit of prestige and wealth. Here is another case in which the confrontation by a stranger is what broke the cycle of compulsion in the life of an alcoholic. Fortunately, outsiders observe a lot more about us than we realize. That is often in our best interest.

The intervention by an outsider that stands out the most in Deirdre's entry into recovery was the simple, sweet greeting by a haggard old man reaching out with genuine warmth and care to a beautiful, frightened young woman. We never know how profoundly our simple gestures are going to affect another person's life; and we never know how profoundly we can be affected by some very unlikely sources of God's love, if we only pay attention.

CHAPTER SEVEN
Robert

*"My old insecurities started gradually being replaced
with an appreciation for the way God made me ."*

At age 18 Robert, a former Boy Scout from a middle
class family in a beautiful seaside community, had
already experienced more wreckage in his life from the
disease of addiction than most addicts do by the time
they are 40. He came from a close supportive family,
had a little brother whom he loved, attended a good
school, made good grades, was a star athlete, and
was known for his great sense of humor.

Despite his apparent good fortune in childhood
and teen years, Robert had a completely different
experience going on inside of himself than appeared on
the surface. He constantly felt like he was inferior and
a misfit, despite his popularity, skills and intelligence.
He described the feeling as secretly being paranoid
all the time. He believed that people around him might
be judging and criticizing him for being "inadequate."
He certainly judged himself as inadequate despite
no evidence of inadequacy. One obsession Robert
had was his appearance. In his mind his differences

from other people, like his slightly smaller stature, were magnified. Coastal Southern California is a difficult place to look too different. It is the unofficial headquarters of the cult of youth and beauty. He was able to push through the paranoid feelings and act cool. He got his ear pierced, tried to look tough, and tried to act like nothing bothered him, all in an attempt to cover up the emotional battle that was going on inside.

Then at age 13, he finally discovered something that took away all the feelings of insecurity and helped him feel confident. It wasn't the sports in which he was so skilled, it wasn't the sound of laughter as he cracked jokes, it wasn't the accomplishment of good grades or merit badges. It came in a bottle and was easy to obtain. HIs friends were able to occasionally obtain it, and his parents kept it in their liquor cabinet at home. Alcohol intoxication was the most wonderful thing he had ever experienced. It freed him from the constant inner turmoil that had haunted him for as long as he could remember. He drank it whenever his friends had some, and sometimes stole it from his parents. He was all the more unhappy whenever he was not intoxicated, but always quickly found relief as soon as he could obtain more alcohol. He knew that his grades and his athletic abilities were rapidly deteriorating; but he was willing to give those up for the good feeling of intoxication.

It wasn't long before marijuana was added to his alcohol consumption, and at that point he decided that he was a new person with a whole new identity: Addict. He was actually proud of that image and actively portrayed it. He tried numerous other drugs and loved them all. He made sure he was under the influence every day. After awhile, it seemed useless to even attend classes, and he somehow managed to get away with cutting classes with friends almost daily. They would just hang out on the streets of the city, most of the day; then go home to their families who were none the wiser.

After 3 years of being an addict, he began to be disgusted with himself. He started feeling like he desperately wanted out of the endless cycle of highs and lows that all addicts experience. He had figured out that for every high he would experience, there would be a low depressed feeling that would follow, even worse than the one before. Sometimes he actually stood in front of a mirror, and out of self-loathing, would flip himself off.

He had been intoxicated almost every day for 4 years. Being without a drug in his system was extremely rare, anytime of the day or night. When he was not under the influence the fears, insecurities, and self-loathing would come flooding back to him. Everything he did as a teenager was done under the influence, including driving. One day when he was 17 years old, he blacked out while driving and had a terrible accident. He was the only one hurt. At the hospital the doctors were much more concerned about his cognitive state from the blackout than they were about any injuries from the accident. He was treated, brought back to consciousness, his vital signs stabilized, and he was released with the mandate to immediately get into addiction treatment. His parents were devastated. Robert had been so cunning and manipulative for the entire 4 years of his alcohol and other drug use, until his parents had never known he had a problem.

As is typical for addicts under the age of 18, Robert entered an outpatient treatment program rather than an inpatient program. He met with other addicted adolescents in daily groups while attending school and living at home. Twelve Step meetings were required on a regular basis. In these meetings he would hear people openly share the same feelings that he had been trying to keep hidden. He was amazed to hear that other people had felt the same insecurity and paranoid feelings that he had battled for his entire life. People spoke of "spiritual awakenings" and he very much wanted to experience that, but he could just never wrap his mind around the concept of a higher power. He very much wanted sobriety, but the cravings got to be overwhelming and he began getting high while in the outpatient program. Feelings of being stuck, doomed, and hopeless filled Robert. He was finally caught under the influence during an outpatient session, and was sent to residential treatment, where he would live in a house 24 hours a day, seven days a week for several months with other younger guys who were in recovery from addiction. His parents let him know that this was his one and only option for a roof over his head and meals to eat.

On the 2-hour drive to the residential center, the full impact of what Robert had become finally hit him as he watched his father break down in tears crying. The emotional impact of Robert's addiction hit both of them at the same time. This once promising, intelligent athlete with a charming sense of humor had become a sickly, dejected, run- down drug addict at age 17. The feelings of hopelessness, and the horror of what he had done to his loving family continued to plague Robert all the way to the center and after he arrived.

Fear gripped Robert as he entered the unfamiliar surroundings of the residence in a strange city, surrounded by a large group of guys he'd never met. After all, Robert had never felt secure about his worth or his identity in his entire life. Now, this hardened drug addict is thrown in with a bunch of guys, mostly a few years older, who appear to be confident and happy. He had always felt like he didn't fit in; and now, he knew he was a misfit. How could he possibly last for months in this environment; and without the only thing that ever gave him any comfort? He just knew he would finally go completely crazy.

Fortunately, first impressions are often wrong. Right away, Robert was caught up in his amazement that people were actually wanting to talk to him and listen to what he had to say. In the 12 Step meetings which were integral to the program, he heard guys in their teens and 20's actually speaking honestly and candidly about their fears, their insecurities, and their personal faults. He also heard hope and joy. All of this was completely foreign to him; but it amazed and intrigued him. They had his full attention. Something was changing inside of him as he would listen to their stories, and relate to their feelings. He also began to feel hopeful for the first time in his life. He was encouraged by everyone in that program to "get honest." That meant acknowledging to himself and then saying out loud all of the feelings of shame, misguided thoughts, and selfish devious behaviors that he had always kept hidden. It eventually also came to mean expressing remorse, hope, love, and joy. Robert began to understand the irrationality of his fears, his insecurities; and how his life had become run by fear and insecurity. He also began to see how he had been manipulative, duplicitous and selfish; and the devastating results of these traits on the lives of his family members.

By observing and interacting with other young men who had adopted an entirely new way of living and being, Robert began to feel hope. He began to try new behaviors; some as simple as being more organized and tidy. He tried honesty, rather than telling lies; although he had formerly even lied about many things that were inconsequential. He took emotional risks by expressing himself more openly. He slowly began to see some value in himself. The old insecurities were beginning to be replaced with an appreciation for, as Robert puts it, "The way God made me."

As Robert became more comfortable with himself, he began to form friendships with people based on caring and support. He revels in the joy of being able to help people with everyday life challenges, as well as with recovering from addiction. He and his family members are all close and supportive of each other, now. They have all healed from the past disappointments and hurts.

Robert attributes his new perspectives in life to his relationship with God. At age 21, Robert sees that God has been there in his life all along. Robert was just not paying attention. He finds closeness with God through enjoying the simple things in life, being selfless in his attitudes, and giving back to others in his behaviors. The three steps of the Twelve Steps that are most significant to Robert at this time are: Step 3 (belief that God can restore him to sanity); Step 11 (prayer and meditation); and Step 12 (service to others). He reports getting high on service to others, and the gratitude that oods him as he reflects on his new life.

Robert's advice to anyone seeking a change in their life is to surrender your will to a power greater than yourself, ask for help from others who are changing their lives, and talk openly about whatever you are thinking and feeling.

Robert's experience illustrates the private wars that rage within many addicts from a very early age. Many people, with or without the disease of addiction have very private profound inner struggles that are often masked. Robert was typical of many of these people: Outwardly talented, with friends, supportive families, good health, economic stability, and an enriched environment. The psychology literature calls these life conditions "protective factors" against emotional or behavioral problems in life.

However, we are discovering too many people who are not protected by these so-called protective factors, especially when the disease of addiction is present in the person's DNA. The person who may appear to have it all together could be living in a state of fear, insecurity, and even paranoid feelings. Unfortunately, people can be so deeply locked in their own private world, and so good at masking their true feelings until it is virtually impossible to get through their defenses. The euphoric neurobiological response to alcohol and other drugs further complicates getting through to people who are not only trapped in a cycle of self-loathing, but who also have brains highjacked by drugs. To break down the walls of Robert's defenses, it seems to have taken a combination of severe consequences of a blackout and terrifying accident, parental boundaries leaving him no other options but treatment, and the unconditional care and regard of people to whom he could relate. From that point, he became willing to open up and receive the guidance he needed to live a successful life.

Robert's experience also illustrates another truth about the disease of addiction: It is no fun! Those who do not have the disease often look at those who are in the midst of the disease as free-wheeling, narcissistic hedonists having a great time at everyone else's expense. After a relatively brief time in the development of the disease, this is simply not the case. In the beginning stage of the disease, they do feel great. It is as if a starving man is given a royal feast. However, after this initial stage, just like Robert, addicts are miserable in their use. They simply feel trapped in the cycle of using in order to survive; because their brains are telling them that they must use in order to survive. Yes, it is crazy.

His healing ultimately came from the unconditional positive regard of his peers in recovery who illustrated for him the profound power of a higher power; and then Robert was able to incorporate the higher power into his own experience through prayer, meditation, and service to others. Now, the torture is over, replaced by self-love, love for others, and a deep sense of gratitude.

CHAPTER EIGHT
Maverick

"I strive not to strive."

It is highly unlikely that a 23 year old guy who has the disease of addiction and was reared by alcoholic/ addicts who were also reared by alcoholic/addicts would happily be able to say that he has 3 and a half years sober; but such is the case with Maverick. A young addict growing up in a home with addicted parents, and who comes from several generations of people who died of the disease typically has little reference to any other type of life, and almost no motivation to change. Alcohol and other drug use becomes the norm. Sobriety is a foreign, odd, and frightening concept.

Maverick grew up in the beautiful mountain paradise of Taos, New Mexico. He was an emotionally intense kid, and was troubled by his parents' fighting. Mom was in her first few years of recovery, and Dad was actively using. Maverick felt that combination of superiority and insecurity that is so familiar to people who have the disease of addiction. He remembers feeling fearful. He was afraid of abandonment, and not being loved. It is almost impossible to feel a bond with an addicted father; and he felt little connection with his mother who seemed preoccupied with her own life, her co-dependent marriage and her 12 Step support groups.

He was also afraid of experiencing his own internal consciousness. He feared finding out who and what he was as a person. There was some deep sense fear of what might be lurking inside. At the same time, Maverick also saw himself as more intelligent and advanced than other people. Even as a child he found relief from this internal tug-of- war between insecurity and superiority by drinking.

As it became apparent in his early teens that he was an alcoholic, he believed that he had a superior form of alcoholism. He believed it was a form unlike his parents or his many relatives who had died of the disease. He believed that his alcoholic drinking would not seriously impair him and there would be no real consequences of his drinking. This is a little different than the usual form of denial than most alcoholics experience early in the disease. Most alcoholics do not acknowledge the alcoholism at all. It takes a lot more effort to acknowledge the disease but to decide that you are somehow exempt from the consequences of it.

By age 14, Maverick had discovered opiates, and soon was shooting heroin. There was not a drug he would not use and enjoy. He had no problem affording his expensive habits. Check fraud was easy. He also stole valuables. Pot dealing was also profitable. He was able to continue this life style until age 16, without significant consequences. Maverick was bright, charming, good-looking, and highly manipulative. He was able to fool a lot of people for a long time.

Maverick had always had an amalgam of conflicting emotions and self-perceptions. He knew he was bright, and well-liked. At the same time he was terrified of knowing himself. He thought that some terrible thing might be lurking deep inside him. He was very self-conscious and did not want to show emotions, despite feeling emotions with great intensity. Despite being self-possessed, Maverick also felt great empathy for others. He also had deep affection for certain people, particularly girlfriends; yet would not show his affection, especially in front of other people. His image was of utmost importance to him, and he somehow associated affection with weakness.

Maverick believes that parenting played a major role in his escalating drug use. Even at a young age, he had no place to turn for a sense of security. His parents were consumed in their dysfunctional relationship and resulting fights. Often a child in those situations will take some solace in a caring relative; however, Maverick's relatives were either dead from the disease of addiction or were actively using. The primary relationships in life were his friends who were also abusing drugs.

At age 16 he went to addiction treatment, followed by three more treatments. By age 20, Maverick was beginning to worry about his inability to stop using drugs. He felt truly desperate and out of control for the first time in his life. At that time, he entered a residential extended care program for men in their 20's where he found a staff with whom he could relate (also young addicts in recovery), very firm consistent boundaries, caring confrontation when he tried to manipulate or let small things slide, and other guys like him, who were ready for a major change. No one was buying his bright, charming facade. This community of other addicts in recovery who could see through his manipulations (the same ones they had used) was key for Maverick's own recovery. At that point in his life, he only trusted addicts. It was vital that people not let him get away with even the slightest manipulation or laziness in his recovery.

For the first time in his life he began to experience God, and he believes that God is the power that helps him stay sober. He "strives not to strive" and to instead to surrender to God to guide his life. His goal is to be a loving, benevolent, responsible and humble man. He tries to stay aware of ways in which he needs to improve; and is okay with being imperfect. He trusts in God to show him the ways to improve and live.

Maverick now focuses his attention on all the good things in his life: A loving relationship; an awesome job; academics; helping others in early recovery; and the fellowship of the 12 Step community.

Maverick's life took an unusual course for someone of his early life experience: He could have been plagued by crippling depression; an anxiety disorder; trauma disorders; insecurity; self-centeredness; or any number of other emotional and social dysfunctions. For some reason this did not happen on any long-term basis. At the very least, not having the advantage of a bond with a loving adult in his early years, the field of psychology would predict an "Attachment Disorder" bringing with it a severe Personality Disorder involving, at the least, strong Narcissistic traits (an impairment in the ability to empathize with others). This circumstance would predictably impair a person's ability to ever enjoy fulfilling relationships. However, he was actually bothered by his strong sensitivity to the needs of others;

and now seeks and enjoys fulfilling relationships. He now reaches out to those for whom he has empathy. It is relationships, both human and divine, that were the key to Maverick getting sober and staying sober.

CHAPTER NINE
Vashti

"Accept and Adapt are Two Different Things."

With a history of alcoholism going back many generations in the family, she hardly had a chance to escape the disease. Drinking was the norm in life. It seemed natural to Vashti to take the edge off her insecurity, low self-esteem, fear, and anger by having a few drinks. There were plenty of reasons to feel insecure, fearful, and angry. There was really no safe or sane person to whom she could turn in her childhood or adolescence. In those days she would have described herself as the "runt" of a large "litter." Her parents were unstable people, and her sisters and extended family were all battling their own demons. Even after her mother tried to improve things in her second marriage, Vashti found herself at age 11 with a stepfather who had terrifying mood swings, from the depths of depression to explosive rage. His moods were not the most frightening thing that Vashti had to deal with in her new father. Late at night, after everyone else was asleep, she would be visited in her bed by this horrible beast of a man who demanded things of her that were sickening and horrifying. Her fragile self-image and self-esteem continued to be further and further damaged. She had no one with whom she felt safe to open up about what was happening; and she knew she would be severely punished for resisting or in any way standing up for herself.

Alcohol gave some relief. In early adult life, Vashti managed to succeed in her career, despite her escalating drinking. She had a son whom she has always adored, and whom she managed to parent until her drinking completely impaired her ability to do so.

She even had a relationship with a man who adored her, and gave all he could give of himself to try to help her overcome her alcoholism; but she gave up the love of her life rather than her vodka. Her sister died of alcoholism; but Vashti continued to drink all the more. There is a sense of futility that takes over at a certain stage of alcoholism.

Because of her drinking, she had reached a point in her life where she had given up the love of her life, her car, her license to drive, her own home; and though her sister was dead from drinking, Vashti continued to hold onto her 750 milliliters of vodka a day (equivalent of 12 cocktails). She tried numerous times starting in 1994, to stop drinking, even spending time at a very humble Salvation Army treatment program; but she continued to drink after every brief attempt at sobriety. Then one day she realized she was hours away from losing her son, her good job, and her apartment. She was on the very precipice of being completely alone and homeless, with the only thing in life of any value at all to her about to be taken away, and maybe destroyed.

On a rainy evening in 1999, after another day of work in which she sat at her desk drinking from a large glass of vodka all day, her boss made one final attempt to help her before firing her. He drove her to a neighboring town to what he thought was a Twelve Step recovery meeting, dropped her off, and drove away. The building was locked and there was no meeting that night; so she walked through the dark rainy night approximately 6 miles home, but experienced no symptoms of withdrawal from alcohol. This is considered unheard of for someone who drinks even half of what she drank for all those years. Vashti had always experienced withdrawal if she had gone more than an hour without a drink. She has not had a drink from that day forward. She reached out to a friend who helped her get into a very effective program in Marina Del Rey, called Women in Recovery. Sister Ada Garaghty made arrangements for Vashti to be able to stay as long as she needed in order to get back on her feet. Even though she had no money, she was able to live with recovering women in a safe, beautiful, large house in the marina.

This time, Vashti took a much harder, more honest look at herself. She realized that she was a "chronic relapser." This truth about herself was significant to her. It meant that she had to take her recovery much more seriously. Being a chronic relapser, she was much more vulnerable to dying from this disease, like her sister and relatives before her. It meant that she had to do everything differently than she had done them before, even if it felt frightening or strange to her. She had to give up her strong self will, even though that strong will is what helped her survive an abusive horrifying childhood. It was not serving her anymore. It was destroying her.

Vashti began to focus hard on working the 12-Steps. More importantly she began to let down the barriers that had isolated her from others. She still felt the fear, she still felt the compulsion to isolate herself emotionally and spend her time alone; but she resisted that compulsion with all her might. She found to her surprise that slowly, she was starting to actually "connect" on a meaningful level with other people, for the first time in her life. This connection would be what saved her life. It was through 12 Step recovery meetings that she began to feel a sense of connection: "These meetings always surround you with a sense of safety and belonging."

At the same time, she experienced an openness to a connection with a power greater than herself or any other human power. Sister Ada taught her simple meditation: Simply relaxing the body and mind so that she could experience total peace for the first time.

This was a life-changing experience. Vashti experienced peace. And peace is what helps keep her sober today.

Vashti also began to find her voice. She learned that it is okay to speak up for yourself, to say what you want and need; and to say openly what you like and don't like. She said that she can accept people as they are, but that she does not necessarily automatically adapt to what they do in relationship to her. She speaks up when she believes she needs a change in the way she is being treated. Vashti is no longer "the runt of the litter," and is in fact now the strong one of her family.

As for the abuses and betrayals she suffered in the past, she said that she forgave everyone, including herself, and let go of the past. She continues, regularly, to remember to forgive herself and others; and to let go of that which is now in the past.

Today, Vashti has a successful career, though she learned that you do not have to work under stress or pressure to be successful. Her training and experience has always been in the field of high finance; a field known for its almost inherent demands and stressors. But, she is not wiling to sacrifice her serenity for any job, status, or large paycheck. She searched unit she found that very rare company in this field which is known for very high stress and demands, and she settled with a company that operates within a stimulating but supportive environment. She is encouraged to take breaks and work at a comfortable pace.

Nature is a source of balance and inspiration in her life. She takes regular hikes on nature trails, with her dogs, who are also a source of fulfillment. These walks help her stay in physical, spiritual, mental, and emotional balance. As as part of her balanced sober life she also follows a healthy diet.

Vashti has also opened herself up to love. After spending years being afraid to engage in an intimate romantic relationship, she pressed through her fears and accepted the love of a man who had been pursuing her. It helped that he could completely relate to the struggles she has had with alcohol, and the changes needed in life to recover. A new world opened up to her and she is extremely happy in her marriage.

The valuable truths that Vashti has learned in her life continue to guide her each day: Be open to change in your thoughts and behaviors; Forgive others; Forgive yourself; Let go of the past; Push through resistance and fear; Stay connected to others, even when you don't feel like it; Seek peace in every aspect of your life; Meditate; Pray; Balance mind, body, and spirit; Speak up for yourself; Remain open to new insights, to truth, and to change.

Even with the strong genetic predisposition to alcoholism, alcoholic role models who normalized heavy drinking to her, no one to support her or teach her basic coping skills in life, and repetitive abuse that left her with intense anxiety, Vashti managed to find recovery. Some severe consequences did not work (losing car, license, home, and her sister's death from alcoholism); and a treatment program that is typically effective (Salvation Army) had no immediate effect. She continued drinking very heavily until she experienced that consequence that seems to be the key to most people coming out of denial: Loss of one's identity. She was about to lose her son and her job, leaving her with no identity as a person. It also took a caring intervention by someone at least willing to give her one more chance by dropping her off at what he thought was a Twelve Step recovery meeting. This simple act of compassion is what started her on the road to recovery (on which at first she had to literally walk for miles in the rain).

Vashti needed a place to go on a long-term basis to learn basic life skills. This was the key to her lasting recovery. She could not be coddled. People had to help her face some harsher realties about herself. In the process she experienced the most valuable aspect of solid recovery: Connection with other recovering people. From that point, she could then learn the many components of a balanced life that have helped her continue her growth as a strong woman in recovery.

CHAPTER TEN
Mike

"My success in life comes through being grounded in a foundation of a supportive community of peers who understand."

The phenomenon of clean-cut teenage drug dealers from good middle class families in the suburbs of prosperous all-American cities is becoming increasingly common. These are the kids you might think to ask to baby sit or mow your lawn. Mike was just such a person. There was no unusual stress or hardship in his life. He looked like most of the others boys his age. He attended school, made good grades, and had no particular behavior problems. He was able to keep up a wholesome image for the first three years of his drug use. It was through school friends that he started with marijuana at 12 years old and discovered the thrill of cocaine and methamphetamine by age 14. It was at 15 when it was finally discovered that he was not just an avid skateboarder; but that he and skater friends were heavily into drugs. They supported themselves through drug dealing. All the while, Mike and his friends appeared to be "normal kids."

There was no awareness on his part that anything was the least bit wrong with him or his life style. The lives of the higher achieving guys his age were of no concern to him. Emotionally he was detached, but thought that he and his friends were just having fun. By the time he was 15, Mike's parents caught on to his drug use and certainly noticed the defiant attitude. A wilderness program appeared to be the solution. These are programs that claim to be able to turn around the most devious of teenagers; but some of which have often earned a reputation for less than ethical treatment of behaviorally deviant teens. After a few months in the wilderness program, he was transferred to an even more intensive highly structured inpatient program for 22 months. According to solid research, the longer amount of time a person spends in treatment, the better the chances of long-term sobriety afterwards. However, even after over two years in treatment, Mike was still as defiant and entrenched in addiction as ever. His parents were exasperated. Mike simply didn't care. The one driving force in his life was just getting back to his unrestricted drug use.

Mike managed to graduate high school and go on to college. He did an adequate job in his classes. He supported himself in school with the help of a medical doctor who prescribed excessively high amounts of opiates to him so that he could re-sell them at a profit. At the insistence of his family, he went to numerous treatment centers for his addiction, never intending to stay sober. Each time he would discharge from treatment he resumed his drug dealing business and his studies.

Every addict who attains true sobriety has that one major consequence that finally gets his attention. For Mike, it was on a trip to Mexico. Mexican law enforcement discovered large amounts of drugs in his possession. In Mexico, prison was the automatic punishment for possession of such a large amount of opiates. His accommodations were in a filthy cramped Mexican prison cell with 22 Mexican prisoners sharing 12 cots and a hole in the ground for a latrine. Crowded in that dark, dirty, rancid prison cell with hardened Mexican criminals who spoke no English was frightening and extremely frustrating to a white middle-class American boy from free-wheeling Southern California. The 19 year old boy just disconnected emotionally for the two weeks that he lived in the stench of that cramped fetid cell, painfully detoxing from the numerous drugs he had been using daily for years. The psychiatrist who had been prescribing the drugs to him was able to convince the authorities that Mike was simply following doctor's orders by carrying such a large amount of drugs with him in Mexico; and Mike was finally released from Mexican prison and returned to Southern California.

He attempted treatment two more times during the following year, with more serious intensions these times; but with no more success than all the other treatments. He still had a skewed perspective on what treatment meant. He still saw treatment as punishment; and saw his drug use as the way of life destined for him. His parents finally gave him a firm boundary, demanding that this time there would be no more coming home and relapsing. He would complete treatment, stay sober, or he would be on the streets. He knew that they meant it; and his psychiatrist had been investigated for illegal prescribing practices, so his only other source of income was cut off. He was forced to comply, or live on the streets.

At the residential extended care home where he was sent, he found a thriving community of guys his age who were dedicated to a new way of living, free from drugs. Younger guys wanting to be sober was just perplexing. Mike continued feeling like a stranger in a strange land. He did not relate to anyone in that environment. After giving it 30 days and still not relating to what any of this new life was about or what these people were about, he decided to run away from the residence. Two blocks away, he realized that he really had nowhere to go. His parents refused to take him back, his psychiatrist/drug supplier had refused to supply him with merchandise for his business, and he had no true friends to whom he could turn among his former drug buddies. Mike decided that his only choice for the sake of basic survival was to return to the sober living and try it again. An attitude of defiance is difficult to break through, and it continued for two more months after his return to the sober living. His peers and the staff just never gave up on him. They supported him, and persisted in enforcing compliance with the behaviors that were expected of him. After three months of defiance, he surrendered and started doing what he was told without resistance. He figured that he might as well just go along with the program, because he was stuck there.

Gradually, Mike was beginning to appreciate the predictability of the structure and guidelines of his new life. His brain was beginning to awaken after being numbed by heavy drug use and trauma for his entire adolescence. With some distance from the only life he had known for the past eight years, he could see and appreciate the major differences between his new life and his old life: Exponentially more energy;

a sense of security; true friends; a good relationship with his parents; a range of emotion (not just anger or depression); the satisfaction of feeling responsible; and gratitude.

Gratitude was his entrance into another key aspect of successful recovery. The concept of a higher power had confused and alluded Mike all of his life. His first experience of Higher Power came through the sense of gratitude that he began feeling for his new life. Mike found Higher Power through cultivating gratitude, and through prayer. He reported feeling a sense of energy within and around himself to which he relates as Higher Power. Mike said that he does not have to understand it. And, he really doesn't understand; but that is where faith comes in.

The most powerful experience of Mike's recovery came when he made amends to the people he had hurt. He had never before experienced anything like the emotional high that he achieved through this sacred act of making amends. It is an experience that helps keep him sober. It helped him experience true connection with his fellow human beings in a way and with a depth that he had never experienced before..

Mike's experience in life represents that baffling young person who remains angry and defiant for no apparent reason, continuing to use drugs while suffering some extreme consequences as a direct result of drug use. It is believed that this phenomena is related to the powerful identity of "addict" in which some adolescents become deeply entrenched. Experts in the psychology of adolescence tell us that one of the primary developmental tasks of adolescence is to find and form an identity. Many adolescents experiment with a number of identities during this developmental stage, but others become very entrenched in one identity and hold onto it like a security blanket. It is likely that his addict identity became so important to him unit he could not see another choice for himself.

Mike finally reached a point in his life when his enablers had finally stopped enabling his drug use. His parents stopped accepting yet another relapse; and his psychiatrist had been removed from the picture. After that point, it was through the persistent, unflinching support and guidance of peers that Mike was able to see another possibility for himself. There was no judgment of his addict identity, no shaming, no threats if he did not change. It was a gradual, patient, persistent educational process while at the same time his brain developed and gradually healed. There was only consistent instruction concerning the behaviors that were expected of him, consistent enforcement of boundaries, and consistent support and affirmation of Mike personally until he very gradually began to accept the new identity that he was imitating.

With his new identity firmly in place, he was able to continue in the behaviors consistent with that identity; and open up to the relationships and emotions that accompany that identity. It is his relationships with his community of peers that means the most to Mike. These relationships sustain him through everything in his life.

CHAPTER ELEVEN
Mischa

"One of the most important recovery principles is to have fun in sobriety."

Taos, New Mexico with it's soaring mountain vistas, clear atmosphere, and abundant natural resources is a beautiful place to grow up. Mischa had an almost ideal life with loving parents and a brother who provided security, fun, humor, and the outdoor life style of horses and hiking that kids love. A variety of friends were always available to the bright charming boy who seemed to fit in with most any group. Mischa had everything a kid could possibly want in life. He was healthy, happy, loved, secure, had a variety of exciting activities, and did well in whatever he tried to do.

There was something else going on with Mischa. He had a secret. By the age of 4 he had discovered a special thrill that he could get. It challenged and excited him like nothing else. He could take valuable things from people, and they wouldn't know. That was a real rush of excitement to him. Stealing $2,000 cash from the neighbor was easy for the 4 year old. He buried it in the yard, and kept only about $10 to spend. It was just the act of stealing that was exciting, not spending the money. He already had all the things he could want. Mom did find out; but Mischa just acted like he didn't know it was wrong. He returned the money, and everyone forgot about it. The stealing continued, sometimes he was caught, and he always charmed his way out of any serious consequences.

The 7 year old Mischa was allowed to drink small sips of wine at meal times with his family. He felt very grown up when he did this. He liked it a lot. It was so much fun, he decided to sneak into the kitchen at night and drink much more. The sensation was euphoric! By age 10, marijuana was added to the fun times. Marijuana became his favorite high.

Still the bright, charming, good-looking guy, Mischa went through high school with many friends from a variety of social groups appearing to most everyone to be someone who just occasionally experimented with drugs. However, the truth was that he was regularly snorting cocaine and smoking crack along with his drinking and his smoking marijuana.

His parents accepted his drinking and his marijuana use; but when they became suspicious that he was also using other drugs, his mother began drug-testing him. No problem. There were a lot of ways to beat the tests: Using someone else's urine; taking supplements that counter-acted the drugs in the body; and using fake urine.

By age 19, Mischa was an advanced-stage drug addict, with very expensive addictions. He had already been addicted for 12 years, before he was even 20 years old. He had moved out of his family home, by then. In order to pay the rent, he forged a check he stole from the parents of one of his friends. His friend's parents discovered the crime before the authorities did. They threatened Mischa with jail if he did not go to a recovery program. Mischa agreed to go to a recovery program, thinking that he would be learning how to stop his compulsion to steal, not anything about recovering from drug addiction. After all, in his mind he did not have a drug problem. He just had a theft problem.

It was a shock when he found out that in this recovery program he could not get away with so much as a sip of alcohol or puff of marijuana. He had been doing those things steadily since childhood. It was just part of his daily life. Mischa was not at all happy; but he figured he would just get through this trying time without his beloved marijuana, maybe get a little help with his stealing compulsion, then return to his normal life of daily drinking and marijuana smoking back in Taos.

He had no motivation and no intension of ever quitting marijuana and alcohol. Maybe the other drug use had gotten a little out of hand, and perhaps he could work on that.

It took about a month of living in a recovery home with other young men with similar stories and similar personalities before Mischa finally saw himself in these people who were identifying as drug addicts. These guys loved the same drugs as he did, were able to manipulate their way through life the way he had, and had suffered some serious consequences of drug use at an early age the way he had. Yet, these guys were loving their new life without drugs, and were embracing a new philosophy of life. They radiated a joy and positive energy that he had never seen. Having entered the house just one month earlier with no intension of ever stopping drug use, and feeling completely out of place, Mischa was now realizing that he was indeed an addict and was powerless over any drug . . . including marijuana and alcohol. He began working the 12 Steps, bonding with sober peers, and his life began to take on a whole new meaning. It was like waking up in a beautiful new world, even though he was still just in the middle of Los Angeles.

The Third Step, believing in a power greater than self, was a huge challenge for Mischa. In fact, the mention of the word "god" can still invoke a resistance in Mischa. He struggles with the concept of humility. He does, however, seek to be humble in all of his relationships. He recognizes the mysteries in the Universe, and he sees that there is some order in all of the chaos of the world. These perspectives help give him faith and hope. It has been helpful for him to combine what he has learned about faith and the mysteries of the Universe, with his knowledge of science. He can better embrace faith as he sees its connection with scientific realities; and that faith and science are far from incompatible. That in fact faith and science support each other.

Mischa is very secure in the belief that He has many choices in his life; and that there is not just one predetermined "right" choice for him. There are many good choices, and no matter what he chooses, he will eventually be led to the best outcome.

Mischa has learned the importance of opening up to someone else about everything, including his deepest secrets. For awhile in recovery, Mischa carried a lot of deep shame over something that he had done, a few years earlier. Then, one day he heard a peer share openly in a group the very same secret that he himself carried. Mischa was shocked to hear someone be so open about something that he thought he would carry as a secret to his grave. He was then able to tell his sponsor this deep shameful secret, and instantly felt like a big weight had been lifted from him.

Mischa has learned to stay open with himself. He is well aware of his tendency to be arrogant, self-willed, manipulative and vane. People have always been charmed by Mischa. People have commented that a Sports Illustrated model would look plain in comparison to Mischa. People do often judge by appearance, especially in L.A. Whatever the reason that he is able to manipulate, Mischa is careful to monitor himself and not allow himself to try to manipulate people. He strives to be honest and open in all of his relationships; but catches himself when he is not honest and makes amends.

At age 25, with 6 years sobriety, Mischa is living a successful sober life close to his peers in recovery. He believes that one of his biggest secrets to sobriety is that he continues to have fun.

Mischa's recovery illustrates the importance of those early relationship bonds, and their influence later in life. Though he had taken his own distorted path in life at a very early age, he had those close bonds that sustained him, and that gave him the ability to relatively quickly recover from the destruction he and the disease of addiction had brought on himself. He had a solid foundation on which to build.

Another observation in Mischa's early life is the fact that many addicts show signs of the disease long before they ever experience the thrill of a chemical high. In his case, it was the thrill-seeking and subsequent high that he received by stealing, not out of any lack, but out of just seeking a thrill.

Unfortunately, in Mischa's case he also discovered the thrill of intoxication at a very early age, thanks to the "permissive parenting" that is often commonly found in the backgrounds of younger addicts. Permissive parenting became an accepted parenting style about 30 years ago, and the consequences are only just now being talked about. Many people in society are now starting to see that parents need to be parents rather than a cool best friend.

Charm and an uncanny ability to manipulate are characteristics that appear early in the lives of most addicts, further allowing the disease to flourish, as the person is shielded from consequences. With consequences not fully impacting the person, they have little incentive to change their behavior, and they get a permanent distortion in their perception of reality (cause and effect). This was certainly true in Mischa's case. Even the consequence of possible jail time did not impact him. He was able to maintain denial until the first two essential stages of change for an addict.

His first opportunity to experience a change in brain functioning and a change in perspective was with an almost forced abstinence. This is something that he certainly would have never chosen for himself; but with drugs out of his system for over 30 days, his brain and body could begin to heal. He could begin to see life more clearly.

What he saw was related to the second essential stage in his recovery. He could begin to see himself mirrored in the lives of his peers in treatment. He could identify with other people. In his basic identity, Mischa had set himself apart from everyone else his whole life. He was always "with" others, but not at all "like" others. He was unique. He now saw that he could no longer isolate himself that way, and began taking the chance to reach out and relate to other people. Through becoming more open, he has experienced a new kind of freedom in his life that he did not think was possible. He was even able to share his deepest hidden secret.

Another very profound truth in recovery is that keeping a secret is a major relapse trigger. Mischa did not have to learn this the hard way.

The struggle to understand and relate to a higher power is one that causes many people who attempt recovery to give up the struggle, and eventually relapse. There may be many reasons for this struggle, but the important thing for Mischa is that he did not give up. He found his own path to understanding and relating to Higher Power, through combining what he could grasp of faith (knowing that there are many mysteries in the universe that he did not control) along with his knowledge of rational scientific fact, which is also pretty mysterious and amazing. The important thing is to persist in attempting to understand and relate to Higher Power, even after you think you have it.

Another basic recovery principle which Mischa embraces is awareness of his own shortcomings, admitting them, and making amends when he catches himself falling short. For someone who has always been highly reinforced for charm and the ability to manipulate, it really can be tempting at times to use those abilities to one's own advantage; so he really has to be self-aware and honest in order to keep from going back down the path to his own demise.

He has discovered another recovery principle for himself: Have fun in sobriety! A lot of very good people in recovery emphasize the struggles and challenges of sobriety.

Mischa emphasizes the fun. That makes recovery so much more appealing!

CHAPTER TWELVE
Brett

All of the pain and losses I have endured have served to show others that you can get through the toughest times, and be sober and successful in life.
Everything that has happened in my life can be used to help others achieve a better life.

Having one parent who is a psychologist is typically considered to be enough of a challenge in life; but to have two parents who are psychologists is almost more than a child can bear. None-the-less, Brett did manage to endure that childhood, and even more amazingly he claims it was actually a happy, secure, loving family. His parents provided a safe secure environment, and were always there for him. He and his brother got along well. Even so, he always felt odd. He was a healthy, intelligent, good-looking kid, and popular. Still, Brett just could not escape the feeling of not fitting-in in this world.

At age 8, his brother introduced him to something that made him feel a little better. It was marijuana. The feeling he got was a sense of escape from the tension he felt of being "different." Alcohol was part of life by age 12. This added a feeling of excitement. He always looked forward to his next drink. By high school he was gravitating to the kids who smoked pot and drank. He found his crowd. He felt even more alienated from the world in general, but he had his own group. All the while, he appeared just fine to his parents.

The alcohol and marijuana abuse continued in college, and though at first he was able to maintain good grades in his classes, he was soon skipping lectures and exams.

Opiates were added to the mix after an accident in which he was riding a dirt bike and swerved to miss a car, shot through a fence and plummeted down an embankment. His back was in chronic extreme pain. His doctor treated it with opiate pain medication.

Soon after, he was in a snowboarding accident, re-injuring his back. More opiates followed. Another accident soon occurred when he was skateboarding and was hit by a car. His doctor prescribed all the opiates he wanted; but when he got to wanting more than he thought he could get away with having filled, he began going to different doctors and obtaining multiple prescriptions. Ultimately, he was so impaired on opiate pain medication, that he dropped out of a once-successful and enviable college experience.

All but one friend had become so disgusted with him that they abandoned him. Brett had gotten to the point that he actually loved the taste of a chewed up Vicodin pill in his mouth. Finally, one day after picking up a prescription for 10 more pills, he decided to add a zero to the end of the 10, to try to get 100 pills. The pharmacist happened to catch on that something was off about that prescription, called the prescribing doctor, and verified that a zero had been added by Brett. For some reason, that doctor notified the police, and a few days later Brett was arrested and jailed at age 19.

Three days before his arrest, Brett woke up one morning, and for the first time in all his years of abusing alcohol, marijuana, and opiates, he suddenly realized as he was reaching for a drink that he had a serious problem. Dropping out of college to use drugs had not gotten his attention, friends abandoning him had not made him realize he had a problem, and he did not yet know that he was about to go to jail, but he suddenly had a moment of clarity about the seriousness of his disease. A close friend phoned him at that point and he told her what he had just realized. She told him to get help. It was obvious to him that something significant had just happened on a spiritual level.

He sobered up in jail, the hard way; without medical detoxification. While in jail, he had his next spiritual experience. It was mother's day, he was in jail, and it suddenly became clear to him how he had always ignored the fact that he had been given a wonderful life with a loving mother, father and brother; yet he had thrown it away, taken it for granted, and deeply hurt his family, especially his dear mother. This was his second moment of clarity. It was Mother's Day and here he was in jail instead of honoring his mother. He called his mother and asked her to help him get treatment.

On December 25th, in jail, he received a Christmas gift. He was released from custody. After his jail sentence, he found a program called New Life House in Los Angeles. He entered for 20 months. During that time Brett was immersed in the very hard work of building a new life: He was going to 12 Step meetings daily; learning to care for other people; learning that other people cared for him; developing a relationship with and learning to trust his higher power; facing his past self-centered and destructive behaviors; telling the people whom he had hurt that he acknowledged his selfishness; and learning new ways of relating to people that were more centered on how he could help them rather than how he could use them. Life was becoming new, exciting, and fulfilling without any chemical assistance.

Life was becoming manageable and he had a new sense of freedom; however there were many significant challenges that that were about to follow his new-found sobriety. He was to learn to deal with multiple painful losses while facing those emotions without numbing them. His beloved grandfather died immediately after Brett had begun trying to adjust to a life without the crutch of drugs. They had been close, and this was an unexpected, devastating loss. Following that loss, a close childhood friend died of a drug overdose; and following his childhood friend's death, one his new friends died.

Even in all of this, he was able to face and feel his grief without the crutch of drugs.

The biggest challenge was yet to come. While Brett was still newly sober, he was driving at full speed on a highway past a bar one evening when out of nowhere a young man ran in front of his car. In the dark, and with no warning that anyone was anywhere around, he hit the young man with his car. People outside the bar had witnessed the accident. Soon police and an ambulance arrived. The man, who had been highly intoxicated, was declared dead. Brett was still newly sober and just 21 years old; but while significantly shaken by what had happened, he never felt tempted to use alcohol or other drugs to cope. His friends and family gave him close support, and he was never charged with any wrong-doing. The victim's family even met Brett and assured him that he had their support.

Brett went on to complete college with honors. The owner of the program where Brett had been in treatment asked Brett to come to work for him and mentored Brett to work with the other young men in early sobriety. He soon had a successful career in working with troubled young men who are making a new life for themselves in sobriety. Today, Brett has over 10 year's sobriety, owns his own house, has a very happy marriage, and surfs regularly. He spends much of his free time giving people his time, attention, and direction to finding happiness in sobriety.

"Relapse is not part of recovery" is a phrase that Brett lives by. The opposite (relapse is part of recovery) is frequently quoted by addiction treatment professionals, but Brett is convinced otherwise. He reports that from his experience, once you have the tools of recovery and have been shown how to live a sober, fulfilling life, it is up to you to practice everything you have learned.

"Apply the solution, and never give up," is another quote that Brett lives by.

When asked, "What is the 'solution?" Brett's answer involved a complete shift in life perspectives, pursuits, and behaviors: Connecting with other people in recovery, connecting with a power greater than yourself, working the 12 Steps, being guided by a sponsor, being open to hearing and doing something about your shortcomings, living a balanced life (work, play, nutrition, exercise), maintaining the right attitude, and service to others. If that sounds like a tall order, it is. Brett says that his new life requires constant vigilance; but he is extremely happy and grateful that there is a path to a happy fulfilling life, and he is blessed to be walking that path.

When asked how he manages the psychological aspects of the disease of addiction, Brett attributes spirituality and a drastic shift in his perspective on other people for his success in avoiding the psychological angst that many people in recovery continue to feel. He stays close to his awareness of Higher Power through prayer, meditation, nature and service to others. He overcame fears and distrust through a dramatic shift in the way he allows himself to think about himself and others. He has a positive perspective on himself and others, while still acknowledging that he is imperfect and needs to improve in ways that are revealed to him in time. For example, he knows that one of his early tendencies was to snap at people who wronged him, and that this is a tendency of many people who battle addiction; but he also knows that he must maintain an attitude of love and kindness, even toward those who wrong him. The urge to get revenge or teach people a lesson is simply no longer an option. He also believes in surrounding himself with people who have a positive spiritual perspective.

"Spirituality is the whole goal, here," is the way Brett sums up recovery.

CHAPTER THIRTEEN
Shared Characteristics of Successful Recovery

To quote someone in recovery who chose to remain anonymous: "You don't recover from addiction by stopping using. You recover by creating a new life where it is easier not to use. If you don't create a new life, then all the factors that brought you to addiction will eventually catch up to you again."

The people in this study came from very diverse backgrounds and life styles. Some were older, successful, sophisticated people. Others were privileged young people barely out of their teens. Some came from very tough socioeconomic backgrounds. There were people who were strictly addicted to alcohol and there were those who were addicted to very strong opiates such as Oxycontin and heroin. Yet, all of these people have in common the characteristics, experiences, and solutions explored in the following paragraphs. Each of them managed to create a new life for themselves where addiction did not catch up with them again; and they learned how to fill the void when that feeling of emptiness starts to occur.

All of the people who shared their stories with you in this book have been successful at filling that void in life that occurs at times for all of us; and none of them had to resort to trying to fill that void through addictive substances or behaviors. The lives profiled in this book reveal many significant factors in what contributes to the success of people in recovery from the disease of addiction to alcohol and other drugs. Each of them has several things in common, from the recovered crack-addicted former prostitute to the multi-millionaire business man. We will explore those elements of life in recovery that the people whom you have gotten to know have in common, as well as some of their individual characteristics.

It became clear after meeting with these remarkable people that all of them had gone against the some current trends in contemporary culture: The pop-culture trend of seeking fame; the self-help gurus encouraging the pursuit of happiness; and the numerous voices (including religious leaders) promoting the pursuit of financial prosperity. Instead, these people all pursue authenticity, service to others, and personal fulfillment and meaning in life. All of them base their lives on relationships with others.

Profound Human Connection:

From analysis of all of the factors that people report have most contributed to their success in recovery the most significant factor in the lives of each of these people is that they somehow made and maintained profound human connections. Throughout the history of humankind, nothing has been more profound in filling the void in life than forming a bond with another human being and with a higher power. The great philosopher Martin Buber called these types of relationships "I-Thou" relationships. I- Thou relationships are deeply meaningful "soul-connections" in which each person experiences the truest nature of the other, despite whatever may appear on the surface. In other words, a haggard toothless old man might be experienced as an almost angelic being by an exhausted faded beauty walking into a dingy room where in turn the old man sees the true beauty of her soul (Deirdre).

Human beings are bonding animals. We need to connect with each other and to love. This is how we get our satisfaction in life. If we are impeded in any way in our attempt to bond, either through a developmental impediment (such as inadequate parental bonding, lack of social skills, or experiences of loss and trauma in significant relationships) or an environmental one, we will bond with anything that is non- threatening to us, such as a soothing activity (e.g., eating or sex), or through a drug.

Every person whom I interviewed had at least one person who reached out in complete non-judgmental acceptance of the broken battered life that they had become, saw their true value, and did not give up until the addict also saw his or her own value. The bond was formed, and from there, other bonds were formed in the context of family relationships, friendships, 12 Step support groups and/or addiction treatment settings.

This phenomenon is captured in a beautiful verse: I wish I could show you, when you are lonely or in darkness, the astonishing light of your own being.

These profound connections are formed initially through an attitude, on at least one person's part, of "valuing" another person whether or not they value themselves. In an attitude of valuing, you truly appreciate that this person has value beyond the obvious. Perhaps it is an intuitive knowing that tells you this; and it leads to "seeing" qualities about that person that even the individual him or herself does not see. This is seeing the potential that actually resides within the person. When you truly value someone you are able to nonjudgmentally accept them and then see all that they truly can be, despite what is going on externally at the moment. It is not seeing who you think you can change them to be; but rather who they really are at the core of their being. You might think of it as being able to see their soul.

Humans are indeed composed of millions of electrons, and modern neurological research is finding evidence that humans (as well as most other mammals) have a sort of wi-fi system in the brain. This wi-fi system is believed to be composed of neurons (brain messengers) called mirror neurons which communicate with other people's mirror neurons. When two people's mirror neurons match, strong non-verbal communication takes place between the two people without any concentrated effort of their own. Two people's experiences and perceptions can line up in such a way that the brain actually signals each of them that they are in the presence of another person who can actually understand and relate to them. It may be an instinctual survival mechanism that tells us that it is safe to be genuine with another person. It is that feeling we occasionally get when we meet someone for the first time yet feel like we have known them for a long time. It is possible that when someone makes a soul connection with an addict, and can value them unconditionally, that mirror neurons are playing a role in that connection.

Because of this valuing and seeing, you begin to truly "listen" to what the individual is communicating to you, perhaps verbally or non-verbally, directly or indirectly. For example, when an addict appears angry as a profound connection is being formed, you hear beyond the anger to the hurt, pain, and fear that that generate the anger. You respond, not to the anger, but to the pain and fear. You are respectful in the face of disrespect. You are calm in the face of rage. Respect and calmness are the results in the relationship. From here, a bond of trust is formed.

Trust is not easy for most people; but for a person who has the disorder of addiction it is almost inherently more difficult, in part due to the irregularities in brain function (e.g. the increased arousal in the "emotional" midbrain, and the decreased communication with the "rational judgment" frontal cortex). Then there are the numerous experiences that most addicts have had which teach them that people are lying, duplicitous manipulators. If they are making this judgment based only on their experiences with other addict/alcoholics, they may be correct. Addicts have likely also experienced some degree of trauma in their lives of using and being manipulated. A certain degree of mistrust, even paranoia, is to be expected. Trust is very difficult to attain after trauma. It can take a long time to gain the trust of someone in recovery from addiction. The effort is worth it, because trust is necessary for the person in recovery, and the results of a trusting bond are miraculous. When a person sees that someone is not giving up on them, and remains sincere in their efforts to patiently reach out in love, eventually trust gradually takes form in the relationship. When trust is formed, hope can prevail in the life of the addict/alcoholic.

Hope is necessary for anyone who is just waking up from the destructive life of addiction. They are beginning to feel emotions, and have insights that are frightening. Shame and regret and fear can be overwhelming after becoming sober. Without hope, it would be easy to give up the fight and go back to using. With hope of a better, more fulfilling life, they can keep going through the very difficult process of becoming much more keenly aware of the stressors of life without the crutch of a numbing substance, while they learn the skills necessary to manage stress in life.

The result of this process is that the person feels the joy of being truly known and accepted for who and what he or she is; and they themselves can begin to know who and what they are as individuals. This is a rare relationship which transforms both individuals experiencing it. Martin Buber referred to this phenomenon as "inclusion": Experiencing one's own uniqueness while simultaneously experiencing the other person's unique perspective, character, and emotions. This is different than "empathy" which is helpful but is a state in which one person can only imagine what another is feeling. Inclusion is a state in which both people are simultaneously actually experiencing the other's emotion.

Many psychologists refer to these relationships as "healing" relationships, because miraculous recovery happens on an emotional, mental and spiritual level in such relationships. This healing phenomenon affects both people in the relationship. Both are much richer on emotional, mental, physical, and spiritual levels. Current research has shown that when a person engages in a meaningful relationship with another person, whether romantic, familial, or friendship, there are changes in the brain which enhance brain functioning. The components of the brain (neurons) actually function and flow in new patterns, thereby stimulating regions of the brain that produce pleasure and a sense of security. Implications of this are abundant in the recovery community, and in research studies.

Well-known research on drug-use has shown that a rat in a cage where cocaine is offered will repeatedly dispense cocaine to itself until it finally dies. However this experiment was modified by Professor Bruce Alexander to place the cocaine- addicted rat into a cage with other non-addicted rats so that it would have some company and an enriched environment with more to do than press a lever to get cocaine. The addicted rat in this enriched environment with the company of other rats, soon lost interest in the cocaine, and started living a normal little rat life.

Humans taken out of their drug-using world and placed in therapeutic communities and recovery support groups show the same changes. They begin to find it easier to eliminate drug use, and to become engaged in meaningful activities and relationships.

In order to begin this type of relationship, both people must reveal their true authentic selves which begins by revealing their true emotions, thoughts, and intensions. Sometimes it can begin as simply as one person just asking for help; and another person responding openly, with caring and humility; not as a superior person who has all of life's answers.

Authenticity in relationships is one of the key factors of success in recovery. People in this study revealed that they found healing of emotional and psychological torture through the open, honest relationships with their peers who no longer tried to put up glamorous pretenses of being tough, or having it all together. Each person in the recovery community admits to having shortcomings, not in a glib way; but in a way that says, "I am human, I am aware of my shortcomings, and here is how I am working on them."

The essence of the I-Thou relationship is captured profoundly in the quote, "Beyond our ideas of right-doing and wrong-doing there is a field. I'll meet you there. When the soul lies down in that grass, the world is too full to talk about.
Ideas, language, even the phrase 'each other' doesn't make sense anymore." (19th century Persian philosopher, Rumi).

The most dramatic experience I have had of this type of healing relationship happened when I was a young psychology intern counseling a formerly very successful executive who was grieving the death of his wife and 2 year old daughter in an automobile accident after he had been driving them on the freeway in Los

Angeles while he was intoxicated. He survived without a scratch.

His wife and daughter both died at the hospital. He had been unable to return to his work, lost all of his wealth, was disheveled, broken emotionally, and had never been able to even cry after their death. After I had intently listened to him talk, emotionless, for almost an hour, I was transfixed. It was as if I had been pulled into his mind. He stopped talking. I struggled for words to give him some hope, comfort, or encouragement; but instead I spontaneously started crying as he sat there staring at me, blankly. He left my office but returned two weeks later for his appointment. I did not recognize the handsome well-dressed man, at first. He sat down, smiled, and told me that after our last session, he went home to his small apartment and cried for the first time; then the paralyzing grief began to lift over the next few days. Since the accident friends, family, and clergy had tried to console him with platitudes such as: "They are in a better place now; God has a plan in this; you will get over it in time"; and even some judgmental comments. I was the first person to just listen, and feel his pain. In that session in which I felt his grief, he had felt completely understood for the first time in his life. He was able to go out the next week and get a new job which he had started that day.

Because of the soul connection that occurred in that office, he was healed, along with me.

Addiction breaks people emotionally, physically, mentally, and spiritually. They need the healing that only an I-Thou relationship can bring. Such a relationship brings a sense of personal value, trust in another human, hope for a better life, healing of pain and trauma, and a sense of connection with something greater than oneself. The sense of a greater power than human power is another experience that this group of recovering addicts have in common.

The Ultimate Connection

Everyone in this group of recovering addicts reported that a major factor in their ongoing recovery is a strong personal experience of a power greater than themselves. By far the majority of the people in this group reported that for them a spiritual connection was by far the most essential aspect of their initial recovery and their ongoing success in living a fulfilling life. As Brett put it, "Spirituality is the whole goal here."

This power is experienced as being outside of self, but easily accessed by turning thoughts and attention to this power. Most in this group referred to the power as God, and had overcome their discomfort with that reference. Those who had no prior religious background actually seemed to have the most profound experiences of a meaningful connection to a higher power (or, life force, universal energy, or God). God was viewed as being dichotomous in that the power is both inside and outside of one's self. All agreed with the saying that is so often heard in the 12-Step community, "There is a god, and You are not it!" God is viewed by everyone in this group as a source of wisdom for making decisions, as well as a healing power in their disease. Many attributed their ability to have love, even for the most obnoxious people in their lives, to God.

Accessing a higher power is achieved through prayer, meditation, relationships with other people, and through nature. All of the people interviewed reported engaging in all of these means of communing with a higher power. Some attributed their success in recovery and life to meditation, and reported having a very deep personal sense of contact with a power beyond human power.

Meditation was viewed as being more important than prayer. As I stated in my first book, Common Sense, Intuition, and God's Guidance (Thomas Nelson, 1994), "Prayer is talking to God; Meditation is listening to God."

The relationships formed in and out of the recovery community are reported as means to experiencing higher power. Many mentioned how sometimes the most difficult people can cause the bond with higher power to grow and develop stronger as they require more than human power to be able to love them and forgive them.

Forgiveness

Forgiveness was mentioned by everyone in this group as being a key to a peaceful existence. Forgiveness was seen as being a state of mind and emotion that released each person from a type of emotional bondage, and freed them to live with a much lighter emotional load of baggage and move on with their lives. Forgiveness of others was seen as being easier than forgiveness of self.

Everyone had been through the difficult process of forgiving themselves. While entitled narcissistic people certainly do exist in the recovery community, this sample did not include those. Everyone had experienced profound guilt and shame from their own behaviors and from their very identity as an addict or alcoholic; and each of them have had to do the difficult work of overcoming shame and guilt. This is another place where a higher power came in; because trying to overcome a deep, sense of shame through thought-control alone was impossible. Shame and guilt reach so very deeply into the psyche until years of psychotherapy alone can be ineffective. The people I interviewed reported a fairly rapid release from the self-loathing that they had experienced for almost a lifetime. They did this through prayer, meditation, and the support of the recovery community.

To paraphrase a saying attributed to Lilly Tomlin, "Forgiveness means giving up all hope for a better past." This brilliantly illustrates the nature of holding onto resentment of things that happened in the past. All of the people in this sample had experienced extreme abuse, betrayal, or persecution from at least a few people at some point in their lives. Not one person viewed themselves as a "victim" despite some horrendous experiences of being mistreated. Amazingly, even the young addicts in recovery saw that every difficult experience in their lives had eventually led them to something good. I especially admired Deirdre's stance on the difficult experiences in her life: "No matter what happens in my life, the only question I ask is not, 'why me'; but rather 'how can I become a better person through this?" I was also impressed with Marko who, instead of seeking to forgive the father who had introduced him to methamphetamine and used it with him, asked his father to forgive him! It was a transforming moment for each of them and released them both from a prison of toxic emotion.

Responsibility

Bud strongly emphasized the importance of taking responsibility for your own happiness and success in life and recovery. This attitude even preceded his recovery when he was stricken with tuberculosis as a young man, and lay motionless for years in bed. He took responsibility for getting himself well, and had no resentment of the medical professionals who had abandoned him. It was evident that everyone interviewed had in common a strong sense of personal responsibility in their own lives. Everyone admitted to current imperfections and to the importance of admitting them as they are discovered. All of this sample also had a support system in place that would confront them about their faulty behaviors. No one blamed anyone in the past or present for anything difficult in their lives.

It appears to be a universal truth for ultimate success and happiness in life that a person must simply accept the hand that they are dealt and play it to the best of their ability without judgment or blame of themselves or others. No one can be happy by using an addiction, a physical disability, or other disadvantage to escape responsibility for their own fulfillment in life. In fact, it seemed that it was important to all the people that I interviewed to have the appearance of being joyful, despite any situations that might lead another person to present as a victim of circumstances. At the same time, everyone said that they rely on the support of other people in recovery to be able to maintain their success. They also share with their support system their troubling emotions and their shortcomings.

Seeking Help

It was pointed out earlier in this chapter that in order to receive the healing of an I- Thou connection in a relationship, one must be open with their emotions and thoughts. All of these people do that regularly through 12-Step groups and talking to a mentor or sponsor, which everyone agreed was necessary for maintaining their sobriety and balance in life. Some emphasized the importance of also seeking professional help.

Hal was especially aware of the importance of seeking professional help early in the recovery process in order to avoid much needless suffering. There are many psychological components of the disease of addiction/alcoholism as pointed out in the introduction to this book. There is generally a tendency to feel insecure, have a fragile ego, and to be self-centered.

Also, there is a high percentage of people who suffer from mood disorders (depression, anxiety or both). There is generally a feeling of being overwhelmed by emotion, after the numbing effects of alcohol and/ or other drugs have worn off. Then there are the universal losses that addicts have experienced, such as loss of a sense of their own identity, and losses that result from their irresponsible behaviors (e.g. in jobs, relationships, health). Most addicts have experienced significant trauma, if not prior to their active addiction, at least during the high-risk life style of addiction. It is highly recommended by many in recovery that anyone seeking long-term sobriety, seek professional help in learning to deal with emotions and thoughts that can overwhelm someone in early recovery. The psychological/emotional components of the disease are a major cause of relapse. Dealing with these issues early in the recovery process can prevent the roller coaster of relapse.

As also mentioned in the introduction, research shows that people with substance use disorders often have misperceptions of other people's emotions, misperceptions of themselves, and misperceptions of situations. Misperceptions are understandable. The more we understand about brain functioning and it's primary role in the disease of Substance Use Disorders, the more we can understand how the decreased functioning of the frontal cortex (judgment and reasoning) along with the increased emotional arousal in the amygdala (mid- brain) can produce some difficulty in perception. There is also the fact that the use of drugs alone can have a lasting negative effect on perception. These misperceptions can lead to significant problems in navigating through relationships, and through life's changing circumstances. This requires reprogramming of thoughts that lead to misperceptions, and replacing those misperceptions with more balanced thoughts.

Everyone in this study had spent some time and effort in exploring the thoughts and beliefs that were dysfunctional; and replaced them with thoughts and beliefs that were more functional and would lead them to the behaviors and results that would help them achieve their goals in life. Psychotherapy that involved some form of Cognitive Behavior Therapy (therapies that involve learning emotional and perceptual balance through reprogramming thoughts) was often the means to establishing more functional thinking. Cognitive Behavior Therapy has been shown in research to actually reprogram the functioning of the brain. Brain messengers within the brain (neurotransmitters) function much like electricity.

These messengers begin to flow more efficiently and begin to follow new pathways in the brain, increasing the ability to make better decisions and to adapt to stressful situations. This is vital healing for the brain dysfunction caused by addiction. Cognitive therapy is highly valuable to the addict in many ways.

Even carefully and thoughtfully following the philosophy of the 12 Steps is transformational in adjusting thought processes, thereby repairing brain functioning.

Thoughts about oneself, about other people in general, and about God are explored in this process. Examining what one truly believes and how these beliefs affect emotions and behaviors brings insights that can free a person from a lifetime of depression, insecurity, fears, frustrations, and resentments. These emotional/mental states are all areas that must be explored in the process of recovery in order to be free of the triggers that can constantly and insidiously sabotage sobriety. Bringing dysfunctional, irrational thoughts and feelings out into the open allows us to replace them with thoughts and perceptions that will serve to help us be in charge of our own destiny rather than being controlled by our emotions, misperceptions and compulsions.

Addressing trauma issues is important for most people in recovery. Most have indeed experienced significant trauma both before and after beginning the abuse of substances. Research indicates that most people who develop substance use issues have had significant trauma in their lives. Trauma does not always trigger substance abuse, but if the predisposition is already present trauma can trigger substance abuse. Trauma produces anxiety disorders such as generalized anxiety and post traumatic stress disorder. These in turn can cause people to try to cope with their anxiety through alcohol and other drugs. A drug can temporarily halt the painful emotional/mental states triggered by trauma and stress; but so can the right psychotherapies. Consistent monitoring and regulating of one's thought processes and beliefs can greatly reduce the anxiety disorder that is produced by trauma; and therefore reduce cravings for addictive substances. Mindfulness and other meditation techniques can greatly reduce the results of trauma. A psychotherapeutic technique called EMDR can also permanently repair the effects of trauma by helping a person reprogram brain activity through a semi-hypnotic technique.

Shame is another very common trigger for substance abuse which must be addressed early in recovery. Shame is a belief that one is inherently inferior or awed. Sometimes experiences prior to the use of addictive substances produce shame. Certainly after a person struggles with the repeated failure of trying to control substance abuse, shame develops. Shame creates a self-perpetuating cycle of substance abuse. Shame triggers the use of an addictive substance, producing more shame, and in turn triggering more substance abuse. That is why underlying shame must be identified and addressed right away. Again, the monitoring and regulating of one's thoughts, especially about self worth, is necessary in order to overcome the shame that can perpetually trigger substance abuse. The affirmation one experiences in the context of healing relationships that form in the recovery groups such as 12 Step groups also have a profound effect on reducing shame. In this supportive context, with shame reduced, one can honestly and openly take stock of his or her shortcomings.

Taking Inventory of Self:

Looking honestly at one's own shortcomings is part of the process. Some shortcomings are simply common to a much younger state of development from which the individual has not progressed. Becoming stuck at an earlier stage of development is typical in addicts. Usually, people with Substance Use Disorders become blocked at the emotional developmental stage at which they began abusing alcohol or other drugs. For example, if a 16 year old girl begins getting drunk on most weekends, she will likely become stuck at the emotional development stage that is normal at that age: Characterized by narcissism and seeking to establish an identity. As a 45 year old still trying to get sober she will likely continue to appear self-centered and still be experimenting with different ways of identifying herself. Also, since the alcohol impaired her neurological development her brain likely also became stuck at an earlier stage, her frontal lobe functioning might be underdeveloped, causing her to make decisions based upon emotion (from the more active central region of the brain), rather than from the more rational fact-based frontal lobe.

Other shortcomings are based on a person's temperament type, which research indicates is a product of genetic inheritance. For example, some people are naturally detail oriented, and in extreme cases might be seen as too concerned or obsessed with and focused on details. While other people are naturally more aware of the "big picture," seeing fewer details. In extreme cases, the "big picture" person can frustrate others with their lack of attention to details and poor organization.

Whatever the source of shortcomings, the people in this study had in common the fact that they all sought and continue to seek feedback and guidance as to what their shortcomings are, and how they can improve their behavior. Most do this through a sponsor and/or counselor in a supportive context that does not re- trigger shame, but instead accept personal shortcomings as part of the human condition. The 12 Step support community is a culture of people who seek to be free of the pretenses of glamor, or other external status symbols as a means of impressing people. Instead, they seek to be humble, genuine and authentic in all of their relationships.

The Twelve Steps
In this sample of recovering people, the 12 Step program was an ongoing means of maintaining their recovery. Even those who had been in recovery for over 20 years were vitally involved in attending 12 Step support groups, having a sponsor to help support and guide them in following the 12 Step philosophy, and also being a sponsor (supportive guide) to others in recovery.

Living a life following the 12 Step philosophy involves openly admitting having the disease or compulsion of addiction/alcoholism, admitting imperfections in one's personality and behaviors, needing the help of a higher power, recognizing what role they play in the problems that they are experiencing in their lives, take responsibility for correcting their shortcomings, making amends to people they may have hurt, maintaining a connection with a higher power, and always striving to be helpful to other people. That is a really tall order! However, each person in this sample, regardless of their age or socio-economic status, was diligent daily in taking responsibility to live according to this philosophy and daily practice of living with integrity, admitting when they fell short, and then moved on. It works for them.

Living according to this rigorous but freeing philosophy requires the support of other people who are also striving to live according to these principles. The fellowship, support, and interaction is vital to the entire process. There is an amazing synergy that develops when like-minded people working toward the same goals come together. The sum is exponentially greater than the parts.

Another advantage to the meetings is that people have the opportunity to experience the release of pressure that comes from catharsis. For centuries, scientists in the field pf psychology have documented the release of physical and psychological pressure that comes from simply expressing one's emotions, thoughts, challenges, frustrations, and hopes. The 12 Step community offers this release every day, often many times a day.

Movements have been springing up in recent years which say that following the 12 Steps is not necessary. Some movements are saying that total abstinence from alcohol and marijuana is not even necessary. Studies show that there are some people who do well in recovery from Substance Use Disorders without 12 Step support, but that those people have found support in their lives in other ways. Those who do not find support inevitably become the "dry drunk": a person who does not drink, but who is so unpleasant to be around around until you wish he/she would drink.

Recent studies are indicating that the people who are able to drink moderately after detoxing are people who did not use opiates (pain medications) or benzodiazepines (tranquilizers) excessively, and people who had a milder form of Alcohol Use Disorder. Those who had the moderate to severe form of Alcohol Use Disorder, and those who used other drugs excessively did relapse back into extreme substance abuse, after attempting moderate drinking or marijuana use.

Despite some people's success at recovery without the 12 Steps and/or without total abstinence from all addictive substances, extensive research indicates that the 12 Step based programs remain the most effective for long-term success in recovery, especially when used in conjunction with other approaches to personal growth such as psychotherapy and spiritual practces. The people whom I interviewed eventually did not miss anything about alcohol or other drugs because their lives were so fulfilling, even though many reported that it required vigilance to remain abstinent.

Altruism:

One of the key principles in recovery is the vital importance of focusing on how you can help other people, particularly people who are new to recovery. Every person who participated in the interviews for this study reported that focusing on others' needs and how to help them with those needs is a vital part of their own ongoing growth and fulfillment in life.

The beginning stages of recovery can appear to be very self-centered, but that stage of focusing inward is necessary in order to correct some of the thoughts and behaviors that contributed to the addiction. After some of this necessary soul-searching has started to have a positive effect on one's experience of life, the recovering person needs to begin also focusing on the needs of others; and needs to begin finding ways to help other people.

The most common way that people in recovery help others is by approaching new people they meet in 12 Step recovery meetings and asking them if they need a sponsor. Thus begins the process of passing on the unconditional care, acceptance, and bonding of the all-important I-thou relationship that transforms and heals lives.

Many in this group also volunteer at community or church charitable groups such as homeless shelters, free clinics, or children's charities. As is true for anyone, learning to give of yourself to others is necessary for happiness and fulfillment in life.

Boundaries:

Saying, "No," to substances of abuse is just one of many boundaries that this population has set. A boundary is a guideline that an individual consistently sets for how she or he wants to behave, and how she or he wants others to behave toward him or her.

People who are successful in recovery have learned to assertively and gently let people know what is and is not acceptable to do in the relationship. If others refuse to respect boundaries, often the person moves on from or avoids that relationship. Not in a judgmental way, but just out of self-respect and a determination to avoid as many triggers as possible in order to maintain sobriety.

There are many pitfalls in the relationships that helped enable the person's drug use. Friends and family members are often primary triggers of stress that can lead back to relapse. The recovering person needs awareness of the signs in themselves that indicate when they are beginning to feel the stress from those people who formerly triggered their cravings for drugs. This awareness develops through professional guidance from counselors who are specifically trained in guiding people through the pitfalls that follow the recovery process. Everything changes in the close relationships of an individuals life after the drug use stops. Emotions, thoughts, and everyday conflicts can all be overwhelming without the escape valve of alcohol and other drugs. Recovering people need help in learning how to deal with all of these stressors and learn how to do what so many non-addicted people take for granted, such as learning the art of compromise which is necessary in any relationship. Everyone in this group of successful people in recovery had professional guidance in navigating their close relationships after beginning recovery, and many still stay in counseling on a regular basis. Even without the participation of friends and family in the counseling process, the individual in recovery can learn all that is necessary to set the boundaries and develop the skills necessary to have successful relationships. Sometimes, that means completely avoiding the people, places, and things that are associated with substance use.

People in recovery also have boundaries for themselves. The individual also knows what behaviors are and are not acceptable for themselves. People in the more advanced stages of recovery have become aware of their own shortcomings and continue to take assessment of their shortcomings. Through this awareness they can use self-discipline to change their perspective on a situation, and in turn change their behavior. This sometimes involves education on what constitutes acceptable behavior; and sometimes requires honest feedback from others to help the person in recovery know how to behave differently than their old patterns of behavior. This is another place where the close relationships formed through having friends and a sponsor in recovery is essential in the success of recovering individuals. Conclusion:

To quote someone in recovery who chose to remain anonymous: "You don't recover from addiction by stopping using. You recover by creating a new life where it is easier not to use. If you don't create a new life, then all of the factors that brought you to your addiction will eventually catch up to you again."

Conclusions:

The people in this study came from very diverse backgrounds and life styles. Some were older, successful, sophisticated people. Others were privileged young people barley out of their teens. Some came from very rough socioeconomic backgrounds. There were people who were strictly addicted to alcohol and there were those who were addicted to very strong opiates such as heroin and Oxycontin. Yet, all of these people have in common the characteristics, experiences and solutions that we have explored in this chapter. All of them managed to create a new life for themselves where addiction did not catch up to them again; and they managed to learn how to fill the void when that feeling of emptiness starts to occur.

This study, indicates that there are definite behaviors, attitudes, and actions that lead people to successful recovery from the devastation of alcohol and other drug addiction. The conclusion reached here is is that anyone desiring to truly change their lives for the better, whether from addictions or from dysfunctional behaviors, can follow the example of the people in this study and begin to experience lives filled with more joy and fulfillment.

The most essential element in recovery is having at least one profoundly supportive relationship, and continuing to cultivate other such relationships through reaching out to others in support and bonding. Also, developing a relationship with a power greater than one's self and continuing to develop spiritually is another essential part of recovery.

Forgiveness was another factor cited by everyone in this group. They had all forgiven the people who had wronged them, and had forgiven themselves for their own transgressions. In this process, all had done the ongoing work of overcoming guilt and shame. Almost paradoxically, forgiveness and overcoming shame helped them take a more honest look at their own shortcomings and continue to seek to overcome those.

Everyone agreed that a focussed exploration of their emotional issues such as depression, anxiety, and trauma had been necessary, and was an ongoing effort. They accomplished this through expressing their emotions, and concerns to a supportive person. All of them had a sponsor in the 12 Step program to whom they could openly talk, and many of them also had a counselor or psychotherapist. All of the people in this sample had been in formal counseling at some point in their recovery. As part of the process of dealing with their emotional issues, all of this sample had done careful exploration of their thoughts, and developed more balanced, healthy thoughts which enhanced their self-worth and their ability to relate to other people in a healthy way.

Each person took responsibility for their life's circumstances, whether they were in a place of easy or difficult circumstances. They adjusted their attitudes to avoid the paralyzing trap of thinking of themselves as victims, even if someone had betrayed them. They simply looked at their own part in bringing about those circumstances and/or made efforts to see how that experience could help them to become a better person or learn a valuable lesson.

Everyone in this group of people in recovery was closely associated with the 12 Step community and followed the 12 Step philosophy and life style. None of them expressed an obsession with or radical view of the 12 Step movement.

Everyone simply saw it as something that helped them personally, and as another aspect of life along with work, social life, and hobbies that helped give them fulfillment.

Giving back to others is a part of the 12 Step philosophy that was highly emphasized by everyone in this sample. Everyone reported that the most fulfilling aspect of their lives was through helping other people attain success in recovery and helping people through a variety of volunteer activities whether through helping disadvantaged children or giving a hand at the soup kitchen.

A life of gratitude and joy is what most people mentioned as one of their primary goals for their lives. Everyone mentioned how imperfect they are in constantly reaching all of their goals; but that they can always get back on track through adopting an attitude of gratitude. It was apparent while talking to the vast majority of these people that they are indeed joyful, and avail themselves of opportunities to have fun.

It was also apparent that everyone to whom I talked was sincere, conscientious, and kind. I left each interview with a greater sense of gratitude and joy in myself. In addition, I was left with a great sense of hope for all people who are afflicted with with addiction. No matter what socio-economic condition, what drug of choice, age, IQ, race, or cultural background, I was left with the knowledge that anyone truly desiring to fill the void and have a life of hope, joy and fulfillment, can have it.

After experiencing each of these people and the generous sharing of their lives with me, I realized that it might be more accurate to say that they are in a process of "discovery" much more than they are in a process of "recovery." Each of them are moving forward to discover new aspects of life, and new aspects of themselves rather than going backward to anything that they are trying to recover.

Anyone's life can be an exciting journey of discovery. Begin to discover your own new life, today.

About the Author

Christopher Knippers, Ph.D. (Clinical Psychology) is an author, speaker, and consultant who spent most of his 40-year career in psychology helping people suffering from Substance Use Disorders, Mood Disorders, and relationship issues find healing. His writing, and lectures have received critical acclaim from his readers, his clients, and from professionals in his field. "The goal and purpose of my life and work is to bring hope and healing to people." (Christopher Knippers)

Made in the USA
Coppell, TX
28 December 2019